REST IN PEACE "SLEDGEHAMMER":

CELEBRITIES I MET ALONG LIFE'S JOURNEY

by

David T. Morgan

To my buddy, John Crum, with gratitude for his invaluable help and with best wishes always.

David (T. Morgan)

REST IN PEACE, "SLEDGEHAMMER":

CELEBRITIES I MET ALONG LIFE'S JOURNEY

Copyright 2013 by David T. Morgan

Acknowledgments

Once again I am indebted to my cherished friend John Crum of the University of Delaware for a superb job of copyediting this book. As always he found errors that I overlooked, and I am grateful to him for his diligence in detecting the flaws and making valuable suggestions for improving my work.

My thanks also go to Stacia Childress of the University of Montevallo for converting my manuscript into a PDF document, a necessary requirement for publication.

Finally, I thank all of those people, whoever they may be, that have contributed to the development of the technology that makes publication so easy these days. Because of their contributions, anyone can become an author now. I know that this is both good and bad, since many writers will self-publish books that might never be regarded as literary gems or even good books. On the other hand, some writers, who would never have been able to get a book accepted by traditional publishers in years past can now get their books into the literary marketplace and thus have the potential for producing a literary gem. It is unlikely that this book would have gotten a second look by a traditional publisher, and it may not be a literary gem, but I believe it contains a worthwhile message, and I am thankful that I can make it available to all who want to read it, no matter how many or how few they may be.

Description

This book is about eighteen celebrities that I met along life's journey. Although among the eighteen are United States presidents, secretaries of state, a five star general, a Communist Party chairman, hall of fame athletes, and award winning writers, receiving special attention is Professor Eugene B. Sledge, my colleague and friend for many years. This biology professor at a small state university achieved national and international fame in the 1980s by writing a war memoir detailing his combat experiences in World War II. His book, *With the Old Breed at Peleliu and Okinawa,* has been called "the finest literary account to emerge about the Pacific war," and has been ranked as one of the ten greatest war books ever written. Nicknamed "Sledgehammer" by his Marine buddies, Sledge was haunted by his war experiences until death claimed him in 2001. I honor his memory with this book's title, *Rest in Peace, "Sledgehammer."* At one point during the assault to capture Peleliu from the Japanese, Sledge seemed to despair of surviving. He wrote: "How we kept going and continued fighting I'll never know. I was so indescribably weary physically and emotionally that I became fatalistic, praying only for my fate to be painless."*

Read his story and the stories of the other celebrities I met along life's journey on the pages that follow.

"*With the Old Breed at Peleliu and Okinawa,*" p. 160. (Paperback edition, 1991)

Introduction

Along life's journey I have been fortunate enough to come face to face with a few people who achieved fame in one way or another. Most of the ones I encountered were people I admired and liked. One I liked but did not admire, while another I neither liked nor admired. Only one, General George C. Marshall, might be regarded universally as a genuine hero. Two were presidents of the United States—George H. W. Bush and Jimmy Carter—and are due the respect that should be given to all of the men who have held that exalted office. However, the measure of esteem in which each has been held depends on one's political perspective. Another national political figure that I encountered and came to know was Dean Rusk, our fifty-third secretary of state. In my opinion, Mr. Rusk was a great man and a delight to have for company. Governor George Wallace was either famous or infamous, depending upon one's point of view. I never admired him, but I liked him very much. He was always cordial when I met him, and he had a way of convincing me that I was his longtime friend—even an old buddy. The last of the political figures I knew was Senator Phil Gramm of Texas, whom I neither liked nor admired, but with whom I was a colleague on the faculty of Texas A&M University.

All the others I met, save two, were an entertainer, three sports figures, and a number of highly acclaimed writers. The entertainer was Kenny Rogers, one of the most popular singers of my time. The sports figures include Stan Musial, my boyhood hero among baseball players, who won a place in the National Baseball Hall of Fame, and Billy Cunningham, whom I knew well during his years as a student and star basketball player at the University of North Carolina. He is in the National Basketball Hall of

Fame. The third sports figure I met was Coach Gene Stallings, who led the University of Alabama to a national football championship. The celebrated writers I met or have known personally include Walter Isaacson, Eugene B. Sledge, Studs Terkel, Barbara Tuchman, and Gordon S. Wood.

Sledge, my faculty colleague for 19 years, is, of course, the "Sledgehammer" noted in the book's title. I had more personal interaction with him than with any other celebrity I ever met or knew, and I take great delight in singling him out by using in the book's title the nickname that his Marine Corps buddies gave him in the Pacific Theater during World War II. A biology professor who loved birds, Sledge became famous by writing one of the best war memoirs of all time!

The unmentioned celebrities until now include the famous evangelist Billy Graham and David Marshall "Carbine" Williams, inventor of the M-1 carbine that several of America's top generals have said helped the United States win World War II. Also not mentioned so far is Rosalyn Carter, the wife of our thirty-ninth president. Mrs. Carter's celebrity status hinges, of course, on her being the nation's First Lady for four years, and she will be discussed in conjunction with her husband.

I propose to write about all of the above celebrities and tell of my own experience with each one, while going a little deeper into their contributions to American life, or, in a couple of instances, I will indicate the deleterious impact the celebrities had on our society. Clearly, there will be many who disagree with my assessment of these notable people. That is to be expected. I am pleased to say that I am happy to have met them all, for each of them has given me a perspective on American life that I would not have had otherwise.

I have wrestled with the problem of the order in which to treat these famous men and women. I could divide them into categories as I have above, or I could present them in the order of their importance, as I view their importance. Finally, I decided that the simplest and fairest way to do it—since I am focusing on them as individuals—is to use the old standby of alphabetical order. After all, each has made her or his own unique contribution, and so each deserves to be in the spotlight without reference to importance.

George H. W. Bush

When I met George H. W. Bush, he was not yet president of the United States. Not until eight years later would he be elected to that high office. In 1980, when he was seeking the Republican nomination for the office, he visited the University of Montevallo in Alabama, where I taught for twenty-four years. I was not a Republican and had no intention of supporting his political candidacy. However, he was a prominent national figure, enjoying some status as a war hero and having held several important positions in the service of his country, and I looked forward to meeting him. Besides, he was a personal friend of the woman who served as secretary in the department I chaired, and she held Mr. Bush in high esteem. Thus, one reason I went to the home of the university president to meet the aspiring Republican nominee was out of respect for my secretary, one of the most able people with whom I ever worked. There were others in my department who also supported Bush's candidacy.

Upon shaking hands and greeting this aspirant to the Republican nomination, I mentioned to him that there were several people in my department who were among his staunch supporters. He responded by saying something like, "Good, may others follow their fine example." I did not bother to tell him that I was not one of his supporters. But I did indicate to him my agreement with his characterization of Ronald Reagan's ideas regarding a solution to America's economic problems as "Voodoo economics."

Of course, Bush failed in 1980 to win the Republican nomination, which went to Reagan. Once nominated, Reagan chose Bush as his running mate, and in the general election of 1980 Reagan/Bush defeated the Democratic ticket of Carter/Mondale. They triumphed over the Democratic nominees again in 1984. For eight years Bush served unobtrusively as vice-president during Reagan's presidency. Mainly because of his folksy demeanor and his right-wing resolve, Reagan became a very popular president, while practicing the "Voodoo economics" of which Bush had accused him in 1980.

Bush's lifetime loyalty to the Republican Party and his willingness to rock along quietly with Reagan's policies for eight years gave him a leg up in his bid for the Republican nomination in 1988, although he had to fend off several other candidates. Because the Democratic Party fielded a weak candidate that year in the person of Michael Dukakis, governor of Massachusetts, Bush had little trouble winning the election. His bid was helped along in part by "playing the race card" and in part by some silly missteps by Dukakis.

As I write these words, former President Bush is enjoying his eighty-eighth birthday, having been born on June 12, 1924, in Milton, Massachusetts. Regardless of what anyone might think about this man's four years in the White House, he is due the respect of every American. He served his nation admirably in a number of distinguished posts and put his life on the line in combat for his country.

Not many of our presidents enjoyed a more privileged start in life and politics than Bush did. He was the son of Senator Prescott Bush, a man of wealth and great prestige who served in the U. S. Senate for Connecticut from 1952 to 1963, but Bush the son was determined to make his own contribution to his nation. At age eighteen he joined the U. S. Navy and became a fighter pilot in World War II. For a time he was the youngest fighter pilot in the service. He was almost killed when his plane was hit during a bombing mission. Managing to bail out of his burning aircraft, he was rescued from the sea.

After the war Bush attended Yale University, where he majored in economics. Upon graduating, he moved to Texas and entered the oil business, founding his own oil company. By age forty, Bush was a millionaire, and he soon became involved in politics. In 1964 he lost a bid to represent Texas in the U. S. Senate, but two years later he won election to the U. S. House of Representatives where he served two terms. Following his congressional service, Bush was named U. S. ambassador to the United Nations in 1971. Five years later he was appointed director of the Central Intelligence Agency.

While serving as president, Bush had considerable success in foreign affairs, especially in his handling of Iraq's invasion of Kuwait. He was able to put together a coalition of nations that defeated Saddam Hussein's forces and rescued Kuwait from Iraqi domination. On another front—Panama—he invaded that country in order to remove from power the corrupt dictator, Manuel Noriega.

In domestic matters Bush was far less successful, and economic problems led to his failed bid for re-election in 1992. One thing that boomeranged on him and helped to cause his defeat was a famous speech in which he had vowed that the American people would pay no additional taxes. His exact words were, "Read my lips. No new taxes." When he was compelled to go along with new taxes, he lost credibility with many of his supporters and was defeated in the election of 1992 by Democratic nominee Bill Clinton.

After leaving the presidency, Bush moved back to his adopted home city of Houston, Texas. For eight years he defended the actions of his son, President George W. Bush, who succeeded Clinton as president in 2001. The elder Bush, often called "Bush 41," demonstrated his humanitarianism in 2005 by working with former President

Clinton to raise large sums of money to help the victims of Hurricane Katrina rebuild their lives after that natural disaster severely damaged New Orleans, Louisiana.

In my opinion, President George H. W. Bush is an honorable man by anyone's standards, and deserves to have the aircraft carrier USS George H. W. Bush, a Nimitz class super carrier of which only ten exist, named for him. He also has the distinction of being the only American president to go skydiving at age 80—a feat never accomplished before and one that will probably never be accomplished again by an American president. I take pride in having shaken the hand of this great man and having exchanged a few words with him.

Jimmy and Rosalyn Carter

I met President Jimmy and First Lady Rosalyn Carter long after they had left the White House and returned to their native state of Georgia. To be precise, it was on Sunday, July 25, 2011, in Plains, Georgia. I had never seen Mrs. Carter in person until then, but I had had a close encounter with President Carter on one other occasion. I do not remember the year, but my first time to come face to face with Jimmy Carter occurred during an annual meeting of the Southern Historical Association in Atlanta. The former president spoke to members of the association and answered a few questions after his speech. When the meeting adjourned, people filed out of the hotel auditorium. I went out a side door and was moving toward the front exit. For some reason, I turned around to look back, and there was President Carter right behind me, moving forward at a quick pace. I stepped aside and said, "Excuse me, Mr. President." He smiled, said nothing, and kept walking—never breaking stride. He was closely accompanied, of course, by two members of the Secret Service.

I never dreamed then that I would see this man again, that I would hear him teach his Sunday School class, that I would shake his hand, and that I would stand with him and Mrs. Carter, along with my wife Judy, to have a picture taken of the four of us. But that is what happened on July 25, 2011, at Maranatha Baptist Church in Plains, the hometown of Jimmy and Rosalyn Carter and the church where the former president had taught Sunday School for many years. Judy and I felt honored to be in the presence of two people we both admired for their humanitarianism and for their contributions to our country.

Let me begin by giving some biographical information on these two admirable people, and then I will go into Carter's days as our nation's president. Finally, I will say more about the time Judy and I met them. Both President and Mrs. Carter were born in Plains, Georgia— James Earl (Jimmy) Carter, Jr., on October 1, 1924, and Eleanor Rosalyn Smith Carter on August 18, 1927. Jimmy's father was a farmer and a businessman, and his mother, Lillian Gordy Carter, was a registered nurse. He was educated in the public schools of Plains, attended Georgia Southwestern College, the Georgia Institute of Technology, and finally the Naval Academy, where he received his bachelor's degree in 1946. While serving as a lieutenant in the Navy he was chosen by Admiral Hyman Rickover for the nuclear submarine program.

On July 7, 1946, he married Rosalyn Smith, the daughter of Wilburn Edgar Smith and Frances Allethea ("Allie") Murray Smith. The eldest of four children, Rosalyn attended the public schools of Plains and was the class valedictorian when she graduated from high school in 1944. She attended Georgia Southwestern College and worked as a hairdresser. At age eighteen she married Jimmy Carter and, though raised as a Methodist, she joined her husband's church—Plains Baptist Church. Later the Carters would join Maranatha Baptist Church, which split off from Plains Baptist Church.

Upon his father's death in 1953 Jimmy Carter resigned from the Navy and returned to Plains to take over the Carter farm. Rosalyn assisted him in this endeavor and ardently promoted his political ambitions when Jimmy decided to run for office a few years later. In 1962 he was elected to the Georgia Senate, and nine years later he was elected as Georgia's seventy-sixth governor. Aspiring to the highest office in the nation, Carter announced in December 1974 that he was a candidate for the Democratic nomination for president of the United States. Winning the

1976 election over incumbent President Gerald Ford, the former Georgia governor served as president from January 1977 to January 1981, during which time he experienced both failures and successes at home and abroad.

On the domestic front he offered many forward-looking proposals. Unfortunately, he was not very adept at persuading Congress to enact most of them. He did, however, enjoy some success. During his presidency the departments of Energy and Education were created, thus adding two new Cabinet posts to the executive branch. He also signed into law the Alaska National Interest Lands Conservation Act.

Carter has been praised as a rare man who dared to make human rights the cornerstone of his policies as president. The respect he gained as a champion of human rights and a peace seeker resulted in a number of foreign policy successes. He persuaded the U. S. Senate to ratify a treaty that returned the Panama Canal to Panama—a highly controversial action. He also helped work out the Salt II Treaty with the Soviet Union and established U. S. relations with the People's Republic of China. Perhaps his greatest foreign policy triumph was his leadership in bringing about the Camp David Accords, which led to a rapprochement of sorts between Israel and Egypt that reduced tensions in the Middle East to some extent. Because of Carter's commitment to human rights and peace, he protested the Soviet Union's 1979 invasion of Afghanistan by refusing to allow America's Olympic athletes to participate in the Summer Olympics held in Moscow in 1980.

A man of firm convictions, Carter refused to budge an inch when convinced he was right, and he broke new ground by elevating the status of America's First Lady. Rosalyn Carter showed herself to be a political activist who was always a companion and helper in her husband's work, but also one who sometimes disagreed with his decisions.

She was the first First Lady to attend Cabinet meetings, and she was a strong champion of the Equal Rights Amendment, which still awaits ratification after being promoted periodically since 1924. As most people know, this amendment is designed to grant American women equal rights with men.

It is too bad that this good man's presidency is remembered more for his failures than his successes. Even his strongest apologists admit that he was ineffective in his efforts to persuade Congress to cooperate with him, and his presidency ended on a tragic note because of the Iran Hostage Crisis of 1979-1981. Unable to resolve that matter diplomatically, he gave the order to attempt a rescue effort that went totally awry. One of the helicopters carrying soldiers who were members of the famed Delta Force crashed and burned, claiming the lives of eight servicemen. Colonel "Chargin' Charlie" Beckwith (a Vietnam War hero), who led the abortive mission to extricate the hostages, said that he sat down and cried over the loss of his eight soldiers. Presumably, Carter's handling of the hostage crisis cost him the election in 1980.

In spite of his shortcomings as president, Jimmy Carter did not retreat from public life when his presidency ended. Instead, he founded the Carter Center in Atlanta where he and his associates work to resolve area conflicts, promote democracy, protect human rights, and prevent the spread of diseases. He has been called into many places as a mediator to restore peace and to prevent election fraud. He and Rosalyn give one week per year as workers for Habitat for Humanity, an organization that builds homes for needy people. His crowning achievement since returning to private life was winning the Nobel Peace Prize in 2002.

Jimmy and Rosalyn Carter are the parents of three sons and one daughter, and proud grandparents of several grandchildren and great grandchildren. They reside most of the time in Atlanta, but frequently return to Plains on weekends. The former president continues to teach his Sunday School class at Maranatha Baptist Church in Plains as he has for so many years, but only on a part-time basis. Those who want to hear his Sunday School lessons come from far and near. Since he is not there every Sunday, one must inquire about his schedule in order to be sure of hearing him teach. In the summer of 2011, after learning that Carter would teach on July 25, Judy and I, in the company of four friends (Michele and Billy Hill and Judy and Charles Hunt), drove from Montevallo, Alabama, to Plains, Georgia. After spending the night of July 24 in nearby Americus, Georgia, Judy and I, along with our friends, drove to Plains and arrived at the church about an hour before Carter was to teach.

What an experience! Everyone who wanted to attend had to line up for a search by Secret Service agents. Apparently, everybody in line passed inspection, as I saw no one leave. Once we were inside, we sat through an orientation conducted by a member of the church. I believe she was called "Miss Jan," and she had the demeanor of a Marine drill instructor. She told us emphatically what we could do and not do. We were not to approach President or Mrs. Carter and attempt to touch them. If they offered their hands to us, we were permitted to shake their hands, but under no circumstances were we to make the first move. As "Miss Jan" continued to bark orders with authority, people started whispering and asking who she was and who she thought she was! She sensed that the audience was troubled by her supercilious tone and jokingly asked if anyone knew what she did for a living, and someone blurted out "prison guard."

Eventually, President and Mrs. Carter arrived, and "Miss Jan" greeted him with, "Good morning, Mr. Jimmy." The former president interacted briefly with the audience, asking people where they were from, and it was soon clear that people had come from a number of different states. All who were there seemed to appreciate the very fine Sunday School lesson that President Carter taught. Though old and somewhat infirm, he was mentally sharp and did a splendid job. It was an experience I have relished ever since.

It was announced before the Sunday School lesson that those who remained for the church service that followed could have their pictures made with the Carters, if they wished to do that. Those who left after the Sunday School lesson would not be allowed to return to the church. Judy and I remained and felt honored to have our pictures made with the distinguished couple. As we approached President and Mrs. Carter, Judy veered toward Mrs. Carter, but the former president motioned for her to come to him, and he put his arm around her waist. She said, "But Mr. President, we were told not to touch you." He replied, "It's all right." Mrs. Carter held out her hand to me, and I shook it, and then stood right up against her left arm and shoulder until the photographer snapped the picture. Judy and I are proud to be in a picture with two people who have made the world a better place. The Carters thanked us for being there and told us to please come back. Even though I would like to do that, I probably won't, mainly because of my advancing years that have curbed my desire for traveling. My final word about the Carters is, "Here's to you, Mr. Jimmy and Miss Rosalyn. It was Judy's and my honor to meet you."

Billy Cunningham

A half century has passed since a tall, lanky, redheaded kid from Brooklyn, New York, stepped down from a bus in Chapel Hill, North Carolina, to matriculate at the University of North Carolina and to play basketball there. A super star in high school, Billy Cunningham had been recruited to play at UNC by outgoing coach Frank McGuire. And so, Cunningham was part of McGuire's legacy to the new coach, Dean Smith, who had never laid eyes on the prized recruit. Smith, destined to become a legendary coach in the college ranks, was somewhat taken aback as the kid from Brooklyn ambled toward him in what someone has called "a pigeon-toed gait." Coach Smith later recalled that he thought to himself, "How can this kid play ball? He can't even walk." Smith's reaction to the young man he saw moving toward him proves that first impressions can often be totally wrong, for Cunningham would become one of the greatest basketball players in UNC, Atlantic Coast Conference, and NBA history.

After all these years I doubt Billy would remember me, but I knew him pretty well when he and I were students at UNC. He was an undergraduate student and a basketball hero, of course, while I was a graduate student in pursuit of a Ph.D. degree in history. Our paths crossed frequently in Saunders Hall, where the Department of History was housed and where Billy took a course in North Carolina history under my mentor, Professor Hugh T. Lefler, in either 1963 or 1964. I was Professor Lefler's grader for that course. Without fail, after Billy took a test, he came around to see me as soon as he thought I had the test results, always to ask if he had made at least a "C." I will tell more about my personal contacts with Billy a little later, but first more about his storied career in basketball.

William John ("Billy") Cunningham was born in Brooklyn on June 3, 1943. He first gained recognition as a star basketball player at Erasmus Hall High School by helping his team win several championships and making *Parade* magazine's high school All-America team. Coach McGuire was well known for scouring the New York City playgrounds and schools for basketball talent, and so Billy Cunningham was bound to come to his attention. McGuire was sometimes criticized for not recruiting North Carolina players. His response was that he could do that, but not if the UNC fans wanted him to win. Of course, the likes of Michael Jordan and Rusty Clark wouldn't be available for some years yet. McGuire had won the national championship at UNC in 1957 mainly with New York players, and he saw no need to change his recruiting habits. Hence Billy Cunningham's arrival in Chapel Hill!

Among Tar Heel basketball players, only Michael Jordan has made a bigger impact on the game of basketball than Cunningham. Known as the "Kangaroo Kid" for his amazing leaping ability (He stood only 6'5".), Billy had some phenomenal performances on the court. For example, on February 16, 1963, in a game against Clemson, he hauled in 27 rebounds, and against Tulane on December 10, 1964, he scored 48 points. I was on hand at a game he played against Virginia Polytechnic Institute in which he scored 40 points and came down with 25 rebounds. Astonishingly, the Tar Heels lost that game in overtime, but it was one of the finest performances I ever saw by a college basketball player.

In his three-year career at UNC (Freshmen were not allowed to play on the varsity team at the time.), Billy pulled in 1,062 rebounds and scored 1,709 points. He was ACC player of the year in 1965, as well as being ACC Academic All Conference that year. He was named an All American in 1964 and 1965. Years later in 2002 he would be honored as one of the 50 best players in ACC history.

Upon finishing his career at UNC in 1965 Billy entered the NBA draft and was the number-one draft pick of the Philadelphia 76ers. In 1967 the 76ers won the NBA championship. After seven seasons with the 76ers, Billy moved in 1972 to another team—the Carolina Cougars of the American Basketball Association. He was named the league's most valuable player at the end of his first season in the ABA. When the ABA's future became doubtful, Cunningham returned to the 76ers after the 1973-1974 season. His professional basketball career came to a tragic end during the 1975-1976 season. In Philadelphia's twentieth game, he was driving toward the basket. No one laid a hand on him, but, as he put it, his knee "just exploded." Billy Cunningham never played basketball again, but he was far from finished with the game he dearly loved.

Not many NBA players up to that time had a more distinguished professional career than did the "Kangaroo Kid." Combining his statistics from the NBA and the ABA, he had scored 16,310 points and had grabbed 7,981 rebounds. His performance as a player and his knowledge of basketball made Billy a likely candidate for a head coaching job in professional basketball, and on November 4, 1977, he assumed that role in Philadelphia. He built a great 76er team that included such outstanding players as Julius Erving, Moses Malone, Bobby Jones, and Maurice Cheeks. With that team he reached 200, 300, and 400 wins faster than any coach in the NBA ever had. The 76ers reached the NBA finals in 1980 and 1982, but were defeated both years by the Los Angeles Lakers. Acquiring Moses Malone after the 1982 season enabled Philadelphia to beat the Lakers for the championship in 1983. When Cunningham finished his coaching career he had recorded 454 victories.

Still, he was not finished with basketball. In 1987 he became the "color commentator" on CBS television alongside Dick Stockton, the play-by-play announcer, and he remained at that job for seven or eight years before giving it up to become part owner in a new NBA team in Miami that would become known as the Miami Heat.

What a marvelous basketball career Billy Cunningham had! He was an All-American in high school and college, and an All-Star in two professional leagues. Perhaps his greatest honors are that he was inducted into the Basketball Hall of Fame in 1986 and was named in 1996 one of the 50 greatest players in NBA history. The Philadelphia 76ers, the team to which he contributed so much, retired his famous number—32. Only a few players have reached such starry heights.

I am proud to have known this outstanding athlete. He was a down-to-earth sort of a young man when I knew him. He was already a big star when I first met him, but there was no conceit in him. He was a very pleasant and likable fellow. The North Carolina history course he took with Professor Lefler was a very popular course, because Lefler, known as "Mr. North Carolina History," had a vast knowledge of his subject, and he presented his material in a blunt and humorous fashion that the students found entertaining. He had strong opinions about everything, and he didn't mind expressing them. And his tests were very straightforward. If a student studied the textbook, which Lefler wrote, he could count on passing or doing very well, depending on the amount of time spent studying.

Billy was not that much into studying. He was at Carolina to play basketball, and he didn't mind telling you that. He was interested in making a "C" in order to remain academically eligible to play basketball. Since Professor Lefler's classes were large, I was given a week to finish grading a test. When the week was up, Billy came calling. "Dave," he would ask, "did I make at least a C on the test?" I would then tell him that Professor Lefler would not allow me to give out grades before the papers were returned. To that he would counter, "I know. I don't want to know my grade. I just want to know if I made at least a C."

What most people wouldn't know about Billy, because his reputation as a basketball player overshadows everything else about him, is that Billy Cunningham is extraordinarily intelligent. If he had taken his studies as seriously as he took basketball, he would probably have made all "A's" and been a regular on the Dean's List. In the North Carolina history course he consistently made higher than a C, and I would say, "Sure, Billy, you made at least a C." Then he had another question for me, this one regarding Billy Galantai, his bosom buddy from Brooklyn.

I heard it said that Cunningham insisted that Galantai be given a chance to make the Tar Heel basketball team, or he wouldn't go to UNC. I have never confirmed that and don't know to this day if there was any truth to the statement. I do know that the young men from Brooklyn were very close friends. Galantai was a different sort. He went to UNC to get an education first and to play basketball second. As was his hometown friend, Galantai was highly touted, and it was expected that he, too, would shine on the hard wood, but he never lived up to expectations. He was a serious student, and he excelled in the classroom far more than he did on the basketball court. Invariably, when Billy C, as he was often called, asked me if Billy Galantai had made at least a C, I would smile and say, "Now Billy, you know very well that Billy Galantai made better than a C." He would laugh and say, "Yeah, I know, but I thought I would ask anyway."

When I finished my course work for my Ph.D. degree, with my oral and written exams left to take and my doctoral dissertation yet to write, I took a teaching job at Patrick Henry College in Martinsville, Virginia. After I had been there a year or two, I heard that none other than Billy Galantai had taken a job as a teacher and head basketball coach at a county school just a couple of miles outside Martinsville. I made it a point to go to one of that school's basketball games. I found an opportunity to visit briefly with Billy, and we talked about Billy Cunningham's playing for the Philadelphia 76ers. It was a pleasant visit with a truly fine young man. Unfortunately, I never saw Billy Galantai again. I did see Billy Cunningham one more time, but, regrettably, I had no opportunity to speak to him. In 1970-1971 I was a visiting professor at Rhode Island College in Providence, Rhode Island. Since Boston was not that far away, I took the opportunity to go with my friend Gordon S. Wood of Brown University to Boston Garden to see a game between the Boston Celtics and the Philadelphia 76ers. Billy played, and, as always, he played well. I don't recall how many points he scored that night or how many rebounds he pulled in, but I do remember that he had a good game, and I felt honored to say that I knew him personally. There was no chance to visit him, and I never saw him again except on television.

Billy Graham

Close to a half century has passed since I stood face to face with and shook the hand of the most popular evangelist who ever proclaimed the gospel. It happened in Asheville, North Carolina, during the annual meeting of the Baptist State Convention of North Carolina on November 17, 1960. I attended the meeting as a messenger from my church. Billy Graham was the keynote speaker for the convention, and, as a longtime admirer of his, I was determined to meet him. After his address, I made my way to the platform from which he had spoken and introduced myself. He was very cordial in greeting me and conversing with me for a few minutes.

At that time I was an aspiring young minister. I even had visions of becoming the next Billy Graham. Over the next two or three years that would all change, partly because of the race issue, which was then dividing our nation and even our churches. The Baptist church where I served as the assistant pastor provided me with stark proof in 1962, as I recall, that culture trumped Christianity in grappling with this issue. In my mind and heart I had come to believe that Christianity was supposed to transcend culture and rebuke it when the culture was wrong, and I had reached the conclusion that denying people entry to a worship service because of the color of their skin was definitely wrong. One Sunday some black people, mostly adolescents, showed up at our church to attend the worship service and were prevented from entering by some of the church's deacons who stood in the door way and blocked their entry. The would-be worshipers asked to see me. I went to the front door and asked that these young people be permitted to enter, but it did no good. The deacons adamantly refused. I apologized to those who wanted to enter and told them if I had the authority that they would be allowed to worship with us. Many people in the church who had been my close friends turned against me because of my stand on the race issue. Word got around the neighborhood and town that I was "a nigger lover," and I encountered hostility in several businesses where I had never been subjected to it before. This marked a turning point in my attitude toward church and Christianity. I decided that the ministry was not for me. I had already begun leaning toward studying history and seeking a career as a college history professor, and I soon became a graduate student at the University of North Carolina in quest of the credentials necessary to achieve my new career objective.

At the time I met Billy Graham, however, I had no thoughts of leaving the ministry. Because this was the only time I ever met him and because my conversation with him lasted perhaps five to ten minutes, I will tell of the experience and then move on to some information about him that demonstrates his celebrity status. Graham and I had in common a friend, a man with whom both of us had been close. That man was another evangelist, Jimmie Johnson. I knew Jimmie quite well, and he told me more than once about his counseling Billy Graham to go to college. On one occasion, when Jimmie was preaching a revival meeting in the area of Charlotte, North Carolina, he persuaded Graham, then a young convert, to accompany him to the jail in the nearby town of Monroe, in order to witness to the inmates. Jimmie caught his young friend off guard by asking him to speak to the men behind the bars. Billy did speak for several minutes, but he was very nervous. Jimmie complimented him and told that he did well "after you got started."

For the few minutes I spoke to Graham in Asheville, we talked a little about Jimmie. I told the evangelist that Jimmie and I were close friends, and his first response was, "I just love him." Then he told me that Jimmie was one of the men who inspired him to go into the ministry. We exchanged a few more pleasantries, and I walked away. I never came face to face with Billy Graham again.

I admired him then, and in many ways I still do, but my education in the years after I met him have made me take a more objective view than the perspective I had back then. The following sketch of his remarkable career is designed to reveal his many praiseworthy attributes, but also a few of his flaws.

William Franklin ("Billy") Graham, Jr., was born in his parents' farmhouse near Charlotte, North Carolina, on November 7, 1918. His father was William Franklin Graham, Sr. Frank, as he was called, married Morrow Coffee, Billy's mother, in 1916. Besides their son, who was called Billy Frank by the family, the Grahams had three other children—Catherine, Melvin, and Jean.

Until Billy Graham was fifteen years old his family did not take religion very seriously. That changed in 1933 when Frank Graham was almost fatally injured in an accident, and Morrow Graham called upon her friends to pray for his recovery. Frank's recovery was considered a miracle, and the couple began having prayer and Bible reading in the home. Billy, not in tune with their new devotion, called it "hogwash," but the very next year, 1934, he had a conversion experience in Charlotte during a revival meeting conducted by Mordecai Ham, a converted Jewish evangelist, who proclaimed a strong message of hellfire and brimstone.

A number of different evangelists preached in Charlotte in 1935, and Billy went to hear most of them. Among them that year was Jimmie Johnson, who was invited to be a house guest at the Graham farmhouse. Jimmie, a graduate of fundamentalist Bob Jones College in Cleveland, Tennessee, took an interest in Billy (as noted earlier) and encouraged him to go to college. That Billy ended up going to Bob Jones College was in part due to

Jimmie Johnson's urgings, but even more so to fact that his parents heard "Dr. Bob" Jones speak at Billy's high school and determined that their son should attend the college that Jones had founded. Thus, in September of 1936 Billy Graham headed for Cleveland, Tennessee.

Attending Bob Jones College was not a rewarding experience for Billy. Although entering the ministry had crossed his mind, he was not yet committed to doing that. Furthermore, he was not comfortable at the college named for its founder, for "Dr. Bob" ran the school in the style of a bona fide dictator. Dating without a chaperone was not allowed, daily chapel attendance was required, and personal mail was monitored. There was no such thing as intellectual freedom in the classroom at Bob Jones College, as professors were forbidden to offer any information that was in conflict with fundamentalist Christianity.

Such regimentation was more than Billy Graham could bear. Before leaving Bob Jones College (later to become Bob Jones University after the school moved to Greenville, South Carolina) and heading for Florida Bible Institute (later Trinity College) in Tampa, Graham went to "Dr. Bob" to tell him why he was leaving the school. According to Billy, Jones berated him this way, "His voice booming, he pronounced me a failure and predicted only more failure ahead." Obviously, Jones was no prophet!

Billy Graham went on to "find himself" at Florida Bible Institute, to commit to becoming a minister, to preach on street corners in Tampa, and to preach and serve in several Florida Baptist churches. After graduating from FBI, which awarded no degrees, Billy headed for Wheaton College in Wheaton, Illinois, to obtain legitimate academic credentials. In 1943 he graduated from that institution with a bachelor's degree in anthropology. While there he met his future wife, Ruth Bell, the daughter of Presbyterian missionaries to China. Billy and Ruth said their wedding vows in the Presbyterian Conference Center in Montreat, North Carolina, on August 13, 1943.

During the six years following his graduation from Wheaton and after his marriage to Ruth Bell, Billy Graham became involved in a number of pursuits, including serving as a radio minister, being an officer and preacher for the national organization known as Youth for Christ, and ascending to the presidency of Northwestern Schools in Minneapolis, Minnesota. By 1948 he had put together an evangelistic team consisting of a soloist, George Beverly Shea, a master of ceremonies and choir director, Cliff Barrows, and an associate evangelist, Grady Wilson. Graham's team held evangelistic meetings throughout the country, and in 1949 Billy Graham came into national prominence when he held his first city-wide revival meeting in Los Angeles, California. Newspaper magnate William Randolph Hearst helped catapult Graham into the national spotlight by telling his editors to "puff Graham."

From Los Angeles the Billy Graham team went on to Boston, where Graham warned that God would not withhold his wrath much longer from America, if the people did not repent of their sins. As in Los Angeles, hundreds made decisions for Christ, and the evangelist was on his way to becoming a household name in the United States. By the summer of 1950 Graham had become important enough to be invited to the White House by President Harry Truman. That meeting had negative results for the evangelist, because he upset the president by revealing part of their conversation to reporters and telling them that he had prayed with Truman. The president was offended and called Graham a publicity seeker who used important people to enhance his own fame. There were no more White House invitations extended to Graham as long as Truman remained president.

Although the popular evangelist had far more supporters than detractors, some religious cynics charged that he was using his fame and popularity to get rich. Chafing under such criticism, Billy organized the Billy Graham Evangelistic Association in 1950 and located its headquarters in Minneapolis. He and his team members received salaries from contributions to the association. The remaining funds were used to pay for the association's outreach ministries, including Billy's nationwide weekly radio program called "The Hour of Decision." Beginning in November of 1950 virtually every American who had a radio had the opportunity to hear Billy preach. And on every program "Bev" Shea and the choir under Cliff Barrows' direction sang, and Grady Wilson read the Bible. Billy was always introduced as the man offering God's message "for these crisis days." The program ended with Billy making a plea for people to send contributions to the association so that it could keep "The Hour of Decision" on the air.

Soon Billy Graham was crisscrossing the country holding city-wide meetings in Atlanta, Dallas, Fort Worth, Houston, Memphis, Minneapolis, Portland, Seattle, and Washington, D.C. When he held his big meeting in the nation's capital, President Truman not only refused to attend, but declined even to endorse the meeting. By this time Billy was ready to venture forth into politics, and in 1952 he promoted the cause of the Republican candidate for president—Dwight D. Eisenhower—who, he thought, would save the country from "the barbarians beating at our gates from without" and "the termites of immorality from within." Moreover, Graham claimed that the nation was running headlong into disaster and admonished Congress to pass a list of rules to stave off its destruction. Congress declined. Billy also said that if he were ever needed to help save the country from communism, he would readily take on the task. Hint—as president or vice president?

An anti-communist tide, whipped up by Senator Joseph McCarthy of Wisconsin, was rising, and the young evangelist rode its crest to even greater popularity. Although his detractors accused him of demagoguery regarding the communist issue, he appeared to be sincere in his belief that he was a soldier for God in battling communism to the death and in his conviction that America was sinning its way to destruction.

Graham was obviously a perfect fit for the 1950s, for he was right in step with what the grassroots of American society believed. His message of condemning evil, emphasizing the family, praising thrift and hard work, and declaring that the American dream could be realized through Christ struck a popular chord. He insisted that people came to hear him because he was preaching the word of God, and for no other reason. Yet, other evangelists were delivering the same message, but the others were not as dynamic as Graham. Furthermore, the others were not as adept at sticking to simple gospel themes and popular social beliefs. Nor were their meetings planned and organized with the care that Graham's were. Thanks to Willis Haymaker, who had previously worked with a number of well-known evangelists before joining the Graham team, Billy Graham never went to a city that wasn't ready to cooperate fully with his meetings. Once Haymaker joined the team, he recommended that all of Graham's future meetings be called "crusades." They were, and they were better organized than any evangelistic meetings ever had been before.

Graham's popularity became even more widespread when he went to London, England, in 1954 and preached to thousands. And in 1957 he preached to millions in New York City at Madison Square Garden and Yankee Stadium. Over two million people attended the New York crusade, and 55,000 made "decisions for Christ." A turning point for the Graham team was reached in New York, because it was there that Billy resolved never to preach again to a racially segregated audience—a stand that alienated some of his southern supporters. And it was there that he ran into trouble with hardline fundamentalists who had previously supported him. They were very critical of the evangelist for cooperating with liberals and Catholics in order to hold the New York City meeting. His old nemesis, Bob Jones, Sr., accused Graham of "selling out," and called him the "arch compromiser."

Billy ignored his critics and became an advocate of the ecumenical approach, declaring that Christianity was about love, not orthodoxy. He said he would follow the middle road between "fundamentalist bigotry" and "modernist heresy." Although Graham moved toward a more enlightened position on race and theology, he remained committed to old-fashioned family values and to very conservative economic and political views. Consequently, historian William G. McGloughlin called him a backward-looking traditionalist and an endorser of reactionary policies. And McGloughlin might have added that, more often than not, the evangelist played the role of court prophet, especially when a Republican was in the White House.

Although Graham claimed that he was merely preaching the gospel, as the Bible presented it, he all-too-often went beyond the gospel and argued for every imaginable right-wing notion that circulated in the American marketplace of ideas. For instance: Satan was out to destroy America and was being aided by godless communists, John Dewey's progressive education, and Sigmund Freud's theories of personal behavior. Graham lambasted the United Nations, the National Council of Churches, and the welfare state established by FDR's New Deal. He asserted that the U. N. had undermined our sovereignty, that the National Council of Churches had sabotaged biblical authority and substituted social service for personal conversion, and that the New Deal had betrayed the God-ordained principles of laissez-faire economics and had thus weakened capitalism. A thoroughgoing chauvinist, Graham called America "the last bulwark of Christian civilization" and insisted that capitalism had to be preserved to keep the world free and Christian.

With the passage of time Billy Graham was not only proclaiming his "simple gospel message" peppered with social conservative values and laissez-faire economics to millions of Americans, but also to people all over the world. One writer even called him "evangelist to the world." He ventured to almost every part of the globe, and at Seoul, South Korea, in 1973 he drew a crowd estimated at a million, the largest recorded religious gathering in world history. That same year he preached in Rome with the blessing of the pope, as his ministry became more and more ecumenical. Once again this put him on the outs with Protestant fundamentalists, but all that mattered to Graham was that he was reaching untold numbers of people, and many of them, Catholics as well as Protestants, were making decisions for Christ. His work seemed to grow larger and larger through the 1970s, 1980s, 1990s, and on into the twenty-first century, as he preached to people in the Soviet Union, China, and Japan, while also continuing his crusades in various American cities.

Not only did Graham speak face to face with more people than any preacher ever had, he carried on a ministry through radio and television, writing books, and making movies. The purpose was always, regardless of the means of delivering the message, to present the gospel and call upon those who heard, read, or saw it to become a Christian by making a decision for Christ.

In spite of his claim that his calling from God was to preach the gospel and win souls and nothing more, Graham injected himself into American politics more than had any other evangelist before him. The presidents who followed Truman in office gave Billy a little more respect than had the man from Independence, Missouri. Graham visited all the presidents after Truman when he was invited to the White House, and he formed a rather close connection with President Richard M. Nixon. In the 1950s Billy called for the election of Eisenhower to save the country, and in 1972 he worked successfully behind the scenes for Nixon's re-election. When the Watergate scandal soon forced Nixon to become the first American president to resign the presidency, Graham was devastated. He had always vouched for Nixon's integrity and spirituality, either not knowing or not caring to know that his dear friend had one of the foulest mouths of any man who had ever sat in the Oval Office—to say nothing of Nixon's occasional anti-Semitic, racist, and xenophobic diatribes. Deeply disappointed, Graham ultimately admitted that his friend possessed a very dark side that had never been apparent to him and that the president's behavior was unacceptable.

Billy Graham's gradual drift to the middle of the road on theology and some social issues made him more popular than ever with most Americans, but he continued to be severely criticized by fundamentalists and many liberals. As in the past he ignored his critics and plowed ahead, even after 1992, when he was diagnosed with Parkinson's disease. He did, however, trim his busy schedule and gradually handed over leadership of the Billy Graham Evangelistic Association to his son Franklin Graham. In 1996 Billy and Ruth Graham were given the Congressional Gold Medal, an honor no clergyman had ever received before.

Weakened by Parkinson's, Graham ended his crusading in 2005 and retired to his mountain home in North Carolina. Ruth Graham died in 2008, and that was a severe blow to her devoted husband. At this writing in 2012 Billy lives on at 93 years of age. Although very old and becoming increasingly decrepit, he remains a national icon. Four years ago, when the Billy Graham Library opened in Charlotte with great fanfare, three former American presidents—Jimmy Carter, George H. W. Bush, and Bill Clinton—were on hand for the occasion. How long Graham will remain with us is anybody's guess, but when he passes on, he will leave this world as the greatest evangelist ever to stand behind a pulpit. Though many might quarrel with what he said face to face and on the air, none can doubt that he said it dynamically and with conviction. Only the most cynical will contend that he did not believe what he preached!

While I came to reject Billy Graham's unqualified endorsement of laissez-faire economics, his extreme conservatism on some social issues, and his almost-McCarthyite position on communism, I am glad that I once had the opportunity to shake his hand and briefly interact with him. I consider that an honor, for I am convinced that our nation—indeed the world—will never see an evangelist of his exalted stature again.

Phil Gramm

During the campaign for the presidency in 2008, former U. S. Senator Phil Gramm, who was serving as the economic adviser to Republican candidate John McCain, said that America had become a nation of "whiners." That comment struck home with me, because I knew Phil Gramm back in the 1970s before he went into politics and became something of a political celebrity—at least in the minds of those identified with the right wing of Texas and national politics. Gramm and I were both faculty members at Texas A&M University, and our respective departments were housed in the same building. We sometimes played pick-up basketball together, and I remember him as the biggest "whiner" that took to the court with us. If you brushed by him and barely made contact while going for the basketball, he cried "foul." Although basketball is supposed to be a non-contact sport, anyone who has ever played it knows that it can get physical. In my mind, Phil was a "cry baby," as we called players like him. He didn't play with us long, and I often wondered if he couldn't take the natural jarring of the sport. More about his "whiner" remark later!

I will make additional comments about him and his transition from the classroom to the political arena below, but first let me recount his background and rise to national prominence. Phil Gramm was born at Fort Benning in Muscogee County, Georgia, on July 8, 1942. He attended the Muscogee County public schools and then graduated from Georgia Military Academy in 1961. Next, he took his bachelor's and doctoral degrees from the University of Georgia—his bachelor's in 1964 and his Ph.D. in 1967. From 1967 to 1978 he was a professor in the Department of Economics at Texas A&M University, where he was considered something of a guru in the area of money and finance. That department consisted of numerous big name economists that A&M had lured away from premier schools by offering them handsome salaries. Some around campus referred to them as prima donnas, and, as far as I could tell, they were all wedded to the economic ideas of Adam Smith and eschewed the economic views of the men who had founded the American Economic Association in 1885. At lunch with some of them on one occasion I told them that they were a bunch of Social Darwinists. One of them replied with a comment that made me think he accepted that label and wore it as a badge of honor. Phil Gramm fit right in with these men (and there was not a woman faculty member in the department at that time) who apparently thought that the natural laws of economics, as described by Adam Smith, must be left alone to take their natural course. No government involvement please! If that meant the poor were crushed in the process, too bad!

In 1978 Congressman Olin E. ("Tiger") Teague, who had long represented Texas's 6th congressional district, announced his retirement. Gramm jumped at the opportunity to run for Teague's seat and was elected as a Democrat. Two more times Phil was elected, each time as a Democrat. However, it was clear to him and everyone else that his views did not mesh with those of that party. Hence, on January 5, 1983, he resigned and subsequently ran for the 78th Congress on the Republican ticket. By this time he had gathered a committed following among right wingers in his congressional district and throughout the state. He was easily elected as a Republican member of the House of Representatives, and thus became the first Republican ever to represent the 6th district. One staff member at A&M who worked in the Athletic Office was asked what he thought of Gramm's changing political parties, and the person replied, "I would vote for him, if he ran on a laundry ticket."

Gramm became *persona non grata* in the Democratic Party because of his unswerving support of President Ronald Reagan. In the first year of Reagan's presidency, 1981, Gramm co-sponsored the Gramm-Latta Budget, which implemented Reagan's economic program, or Reaganomics, as it was popularly called. Not long after his re-election to the House in 1982, Gramm was removed from the House Budget Committee for supporting Reagan's tax cuts, prompting him to resign his seat in January only to win it back as a Republican in a special election five weeks later.

In 1984 Gramm ran for the U. S. Senate in the Republican primary and defeated Ron Paul and several other candidates. In the general election he trounced Democratic candidate Lloyd Benson 58.5 % to 41.5% and became the first U. S. Senate candidate in Texas history to receive over three million votes.

By 1989 Gramm was a member of the Senate Budget Committee and remained on it until he left office in 2002. Before he was appointed to that prestigious committee, he played a key role in the passage of the Gramm-Rudman-Hollings Balanced Budget Act, a law providing for automatic budget cuts in federal spending if deficit reduction targets were not met. That law was passed in 1985, and a revised version of it was enacted in 1987, but neither of those acts resulted in a balanced budget.

From 1995 to 2000 Gramm was chairman of the Senate Committee on Banking, Housing and Urban Affairs. While serving as chairman of that committee, he spearheaded efforts to pass laws deregulating banking. The Gramm-Leach-Bliley Act of 1999 effectively repealed the Glass-Steagall Banking Act of 1933 that had separated banking, insurance, and brokerage activities and prevented excessive speculation on credit for almost nine decades. Why President Bill Clinton signed the new legislation is a mystery, because it was destined to lead to financial and economic misery for the United States in less than ten years. When the financial markets tanked in 2008, Gramm denied that the law he had sponsored and Clinton had signed had anything to do with the financial crisis. However, Paul Krugman, winner of the Nobel Prize for Economics in 2008, described Gramm as the "high priest of deregulation" and named him as the number two person responsible for the crisis, while naming Alan Greenspan, chairman of the Federal Reserve Board, as the number one culprit. CNN named Gramm as number seven in the list of the ten most responsible people for that disaster.

Before his Senate career ended, Phil Gramm ran for U. S. president in the Republican primaries of 1996. Although doomed from the start because of his extremism, Gramm made considerable noise during his campaign and won some support. Douglas Holmes, a cousin of mine and a lawyer, told me he liked what Phil had to say about welfare: "Those who have been riding free in the wagon need to get out and help push the wagon." Others had liked an earlier comment he had made regarding health care reform: "If my mama is sick, I want her to see a doctor, not a bureaucrat." Ultimately, Gramm simply could not impress enough people in his own party to get the nomination. It went to Senator Bob Dole of Kansas, who was easily defeated in the general election by President Clinton.

Gramm's abortive effort to win the Republican nomination for president was not his last public hurrah. In 2008 he became Republican presidential candidate John McCain's economic adviser, only to create problems for the campaign by ill-advisedly asserting that there was no recession and that America had become a nation of "whiners." McCain renounced the remark, but Gramm, insisting that "every word of it was true," refused to retract the statement and resigned from the campaign.

After Gramm had left the Senate in 2002 he had joined UBSAG as a vice chairman of the investment banking division. UBSAG is a Swiss global financial services company headquartered in Basel and Zurich, Switzerland. Created by a merger in 1997 of Union Bank of Switzerland and Swiss Bank, it operates in fifty countries and is the world's second largest manager of private wealth assets. It has a major presence in the United States with headquarters in New York City.

As far as I can determine, Phil lives today in Helotes, outside San Antonio, Texas. An interesting footnote to his career as the representative of Texas's 6th congressional district is that his old seat is held today by Joe Barton, a man who accused President Barack Obama of "a shake down," when Obama made BP Oil Company pledge twenty billion dollars to clean up the mess it made in the 2010 Gulf Oil spill. I would say that the spirit of Phil Gramm lives on in the 6th congressional district.

Now for some closing observations about Phil Gramm: I wish I could say that it was a pleasure knowing him four decades ago, but, alas, I cannot. When I think of Phil then and later, when he came into prominence as a shrill voice of right-wing politics, I am reminded of a story I heard Frank Vandiver, a great historian and biographer, tell in a speech about his research for writing a biography of General John J. Pershing. While doing that research on Pershing, Vandiver sought and got an interview with General Douglas MacArthur, who had once served under Pershing. Immediately after thanking MacArthur for granting the interview, the great general told Vandiver that he was welcome, and followed that by saying, "I do not know what I can tell you about General Pershing, sir. I did not like the son-of-a-bitch when I knew him, and I do not like him now." Similar thoughts enter my mind when I think of Phil Gramm.

Candidly, I never dreamed that Phil would one day become a famous politician and certainly not one who would gain enough prominence to seek any political party's nomination to run for president of the United States. Not only did I teach in the same building with him at Texas A&M University, but we were also neighbors, living two blocks from each other in Bryan, Texas. When I say that we were neighbors, I do not mean to imply that we interacted in a neighborly fashion. I never saw the inside of his house, nor he mine, but the neighborhood buzzed with rumors about Phil. Not knowing which ones, if any, were true, I will not repeat them here. What I do know is that the few times I did interact with Phil caused me to develop a very negative view of him. From my perspective he was condescending, cynical, obnoxious, and supercilious. I was almost in disbelief in 1978 when I learned that he had run for Congress and won the seat that Olin Teague had held with honor. The only people I could imagine Phil appealing to were disgruntled people who hated government involvement of any kind in American society. On the other hand, I was not the least bit surprised several years later to learn that he had jumped on the Reaganomics bandwagon and was loudly beating a drum for "supply-side" economics. After all, that's who he and the other economists in the Texas A&M University's Department of Economics were.

As General MacArthur said of General Pershing, I say of Phil Gramm: I did not like him when I knew him, and I do not like him now. Actually, I like him far less now than I did then. Yet, I am glad I crossed paths with him for a few years, for knowing Phil has taught me that I read people pretty well—even those who achieve celebrity status. When I think about Phil calling Americans "whiners," my memory takes me back to a gymnasium at A&M and an economics professor who frequently cried "foul" when someone made incidental contact with him in a pick-up basketball game!

Walter Isaacson

One of the great journalists and biographers of our time is Walter Isaacson, whom I met once. I had the pleasure of meeting and exchanging a few pleasantries with this outstanding man in his office located in the Time-Warner Building in New York City. It was the spring of 2001, and Isaacson was managing editor of *Time* magazine at the time. I will recount the details of our meeting below, but first some information about Isaacson's rise to celebrity status.

Walter Isaacson was born May 20, 1952, in New Orleans, Louisiana. He earned his bachelor's degree in history and literature at Harvard University in 1974. Awarded a Rhodes scholarship, he attended Pembroke College at Oxford University and read philosophy, politics, and economics.

An excellent educational background led Isaacson into an impressive career in journalism, which began with *The Sunday Times* of London and later with the *New Orleans Picayune.* In 1978 he became a political correspondent for *Time* magazine, eventually becoming *Time's* fourteenth editor in 1996. From that position he went on to become chairman and chief executive officer of CNN. A couple of years after I met him, he became chief executive officer of Aspen Institute in 2003, which is an educational and policy studies organization that declares its mission to be promoting leadership "based on enduring values" and offering "a nonpartisan venue for dealing with critical issues." The Institute has campuses in Aspen, Colorado, and on Maryland's Eastern Shore. It also maintains offices in New York City and has an international network of partners. For sharing ideas and solving problems, the Institute serves as sponsor of seminars and public conferences.

Isaacson has served on the boards of some of America's most prominent institutions—United Airlines, Tulane University, Harvard University, the Bloomberg Family Foundation, and the Society of American Historians. He has been appointed to state, national, and international boards by governors, Presidents Barack Obama and George W. Bush, and by Secretary of State Hillary Clinton. For example, President Obama appointed him in 2009 to be chairman of the Broadcasting Board of Governors, which runs the Voice of America and Radio Free Europe, a post he held for three years. In 2012 Isaacson was selected by *Time* magazine as one of the most influential people in the world.

How he found the time to do it is a mystery, but Isaacson has written biographies of Henry Kissinger, Albert Einstein, Benjamin Franklin, and, most recently, Steve Jobs. Currently, this busy and important man lives with his wife and daughter in Washington, D.C.

I crossed paths with Walter Isaacson, as noted above, when he was managing editor of *Time* magazine. He was in the process of writing his biography of Benjamin Franklin, and both he and I were asked to be a part of a Public Broadcasting System special about Franklin. PBS was using Middlemarch Films to produce this documentary of America's first great writer, inventor, and statesman. I was invited to participate because of my work on Franklin entitled, *The Devious Dr. Franklin, Colonial Agent: Benjamin Franklin's Years in London.*

On one occasion, before I met Isaacson, I had journeyed to the offices of Middlemarch Films for discussions with a number of scholars about what to include in the documentary. Some fine scholars were present, including Claude-Ann Lopez, one of the world's most knowledgeable people on the subject. I had met her one time before that when doing research at the Benjamin

Franklin Collection at the Yale University Library. There were others present with similar credentials.

When Ron Blumer of the Middlemarch staff invited me back in 2001 for a taped interview, there was a fortuitous turn of events. I was told that I would not be interviewed in the Middlemarch studio after all, but in uptown Manhattan at the Time Warner Building. It turned out that Walter Isaacson had agreed to be interviewed in the morning before my interview in the afternoon. He insisted that the Middlemarch staff interview him in HIS offices. They told him that would present a problem because they had to interview "a guy from Alabama" that afternoon, and they would not have time to take their equipment back to the Middlemarch studio. I was told that Isaacson said, "No problem. Interview him here after you interview me."

As the staff was readying me for the interview, I was told that Walter Isaacson had read my book and wanted to meet me. Asked if that was all right, I, of course, said, "Certainly." I really knew nothing about him at the time, but I felt honored that the managing editor of *Time* magazine wanted to meet me. Isaacson entered the room, shook hands with me, and said he enjoyed reading my book. As already noted, we exchanged pleasantries before I thanked him for letting us use his quarters, and he returned to his work.

Since that day, just a few months before the tragedy of "9//11", I have read Walter Isaacson's biography of Benjamin Franklin, a very fine work. I know a great deal more about Isaacson now, and I am delighted that I was privileged to meet this impressive giant of the literary world.

General George C. Marshall, Jr.

At age fifteen I was a ticket taker and an usher at the Colony Theater in Fayetteville, North Carolina. I probably thought I knew everything at the time, but I had occasion to learn one night that I was far from omniscient. The Colony's assistant manager, Delores Kelly, excitedly told me and everyone who worked in the theater that "General Marshall" was coming. She was more than excited about it; she was ecstatic, and she was anxious that all of us must do everything just so for the occasion. Did I ever get an ear full when I asked her who General Marshall was! She gave me a quick lecture, assuring me that the general was one of the most important men of our time. I already knew, since I grew up ten miles from Fort Bragg, that generals were very important people, but I thought that Marshall was simply one of many. Miss Kelly told me in no uncertain terms that Marshall was no ordinary general. She explained that not only was he a five-star general who had played a key part in our winning World War II, he had also been secretary of state and architect of the Marshall Plan. Of course, I was impressed, but not nearly as impressed as she thought I should be.

She told me that when General Marshall and his guests arrived that I should take his tickets and say, "Good evening, General Marshall, how are you this evening?" and welcome him to the Colony Theater. "Yes, m'am," I replied, and I did as I was told. As soon as General Marshall, his wife, a couple who accompanied them, and two Secret Service men passed the ticket stand, the general and his entourage were greeted by Miss Kelly, as I recall. This same scene was repeated several more times during the time I worked at the theater, for General Marshall had retired to Pinehurst, North Carolina, forty or so miles away, and our theater was among the nicer places of entertainment for him to patronize. Fayetteville was the only city of any size near Pinehurst. I said the same thing every time I took the general's tickets, and his reply was always the same: "I am fine, son. How are you?" And I always answered as Miss Kelly told me to, "I am fine, too, General Marshall, we are honored to have you with us again."

It would be many years later before I realized how honored I was to have the opportunity to speak to this great man, not once but several times. When I grew up, so to speak, and became a historian, I learned just what a significant part George C. Marshall, Jr., had played in the history of our country. Would that I could have known and appreciated his contributions at that time! Would that I could have told him what a high honor it was to see and speak to him, a man whose contributions to our country were right up there with the nation's greatest statesmen and greatest military leaders! It was a once-in-a-lifetime opportunity, and I let it go by me.

Let me recount for you why General Marshall deserves to be in the pantheon of America's greatest leaders. Marshall began life in Uniontown, Pennsylvania, being born there on December 31, 1880. He attended the town's elementary school and proved to be a poor student, at least compared to his older siblings—his sister Marie and his brother Stuart. He excelled in only one subject, and that was history. He lagged behind in all the others.

No doubt George C. Marshall, Jr., could have taken a place in his father's prosperous coal business, but he decided that he wanted to be a soldier. In 1897, at age sixteen, he was enrolled at Virginia Military Institute, in spite of his older brother's objections. Stuart had already graduated from VMI, and, fearing that his younger brother would disgrace the family as a VMI student, he pleaded in vain with their mother to hold him back.

Young Marshall went off to VMI determined to gain respect, and there were two avenues for achieving that. He could do it by displaying academic excellence or by becoming a "soldier in training." He chose the latter, and he became a top military student and a model soldier. After his graduation from VMI in 1901, he was commissioned a 2nd lieutenant in the U. S. Army during the following year. Working his way up through the ranks, he was promoted in 1918 to the headquarters of the American Expeditionary Force, where he worked closely with his mentor, General John J. Pershing. He was a key planner of the Saint Mihiel and Meuse-Argonne offensives of 1918, the operations that led to the defeat of the German forces in World War I. In 1919 he became aide-de-camp to General Pershing and remained in that job until 1924.

By October 1936 Marshall was a brigadier general. President Franklin D. Roosevelt was sufficiently impressed by Marshall's work that he nominated him for Army Chief of Staff in 1939. He was sworn in at that position on September 1, the day that Adolf Hitler sent the German army into Poland and ignited World War II. Marshall's star rose to towering heights during the war, as he organized the largest military expansion in U. S. history. He was instrumental in preparing the U. S. Army and Air Force for June 6, 1944, or D-Day, the invasion that led to the destruction of Hitler's German army. In December of that year Marshall became a five star general and General of the Army.

President Harry Truman perceived that Marshall had diplomatic as well as military skills and sent him to China in 1945 to try to bring together in a coalition government the Nationalist and Communist parties, led respectively by Chiang Kai-shek and Mao Tse-tung. After staying there a year and making no progress, Marshall pronounced a plague on both their houses and left.

A year after Marshall returned from China, President Truman appointed him secretary of state, a position he held until 1949. While in that office, the general developed the Marshall Plan for saving war ravaged Western Europe from a communist takeover. The plan called for sending American dollars to promote Europe's recovery and stability, which was crucial to our own economic growth. An effort was made to include Eastern Europe in the plan, but Joseph Stalin, dictator of the Soviet Union, emphatically declined the offer. This led to Europe's division into two hostile camps and brought on what came to be called the Cold War.

The Western European nations soon feared that the communist threat from Eastern Europe and the Soviet Union might lead to their being taken over, and they looked westward for their security. Secretary Marshall and leaders from other nations promptly formed the North Atlantic Treaty Organization to deal with the threat. NATO provided a balance of power in Europe that endured until the Cold War ended about forty years later.

By 1950 Marshall was secretary of defense, and it fell to him to deal with the invasion of South Korea by North Korean communist forces. He helped create an international force under the United Nations to repel the North Korean invaders and preserve South Korea as a country. That objective was finally achieved by an armistice in 1953 after Dwight D. Eisenhower was elected to the presidency.

For his exhaustive efforts to thwart aggression and promote peace, Marshall was awarded the Nobel Peace Prize in 1953. Six years after that, on October 16, 1959, General George C. Marshall died. President Eisenhower ordered that our nation's flag be flown at half-staff on all public buildings in the District of Columbia, except the Capitol, and at all military posts and naval stations in the United States and at all American facilities abroad until after Marshall was buried. The burial took place on October 20 in Arlington National Cemetery. Labeled a "Special Military Funeral," the arrangements were worked out between Major General Charles K. Gailey, Commanding General of the Military District of Washington, and Katherine T. Brown Marshall, the general's widow. Because Marshall had a "Spartan concept of propriety," the funeral rites were some of the simplest ever conducted for a man of Marshall's rank and prestige.

Less than six months after Marshall was laid to rest at Arlington, on March 15, 1960, President Eisenhower announced that the space complex at Redstone Arsenal in Huntsville, Alabama, would henceforth be known as the George C. Marshall Space Flight Center. A formal dedication ceremony was held at the site on September 8, 1960. Eisenhower, who had served under Marshall and regarded him as one the greatest men America had produced, was on hand for the occasion, and he and the general's widow unveiled a bust of the great military leader and statesman.

If only I could see General Marshall today, as I did when I was a teenager, and hear him say, "I am fine, son. How are you?" Knowing what I know now about this great man, I would say, "I am so honored to meet you, Sir. I am a historian. I know of your monumental contributions to our country, and it pleases me so much to know that you and I share a love of history. God bless you General Marshall."

Stan Musial

In his heyday, when he wore a St. Louis Cardinals baseball uniform, he was often referred to as "Stan the Man." And what a man Stanley Frank Musial was in my eyes, when I was approaching my teen years and when I checked the newspaper daily to see how many hits Musial had chalked up the previous day or night. It was indeed a rare occasion when he didn't have one or more, because he was one of the most consistent hitters ever to wear a major league uniform. Seven times he won the National League batting title, and during a career that spanned over twenty years he had 3,630 hits—fourth all-time and first for the most hits with the same team.

Although my interest in baseball waned in my adult years, I never stopped admiring Stan Musial. I never ceased wanting to meet this man whom I had idolized as a boy of thirteen, when I was bat boy for my hometown professional team, the Fayetteville Athletics. And one night my dream of meeting him came true, after several failed attempts to do so. I met my boyhood hero in St. Louis at Stan's restaurant—Stan Musial and Biggie's—which Musial owned with Julius "Biggie" Garagnani. I had gone there to eat several times before that night, but Stan was either not coming in that night, or he had just left. Finally, though, one night when I asked if Stan was in, I was told that he was in the office and would be out soon. "Just keep an eye on the front here," an employee told me, "and you will see him when he comes out." After being seated at a table where I could do just that, I constantly glanced at the place where I was told that Stan could soon be seen. Within minutes, I saw him, and I quickly rushed up to meet him.

More about that delightful experience later, but first I will offer information about "Stan the Man," clearly one of baseball's all-time greats. He was born in Donora, Pennsylvania, on November 21, 1920. His father was a short, Polish immigrant named Lukasz Musial. His mother, Mary Lancos, on the other hand, was close to six feet tall. She was the daughter of Czech immigrants. In his growing-up years Stan was called by a Polish nickname, Stasha, which was eventually shortened to Stash. At school Stash Musial was an average student, but he had a winning personality and was popular with nearly everyone. He had little interest in academics. Playing sports was his passion, and he excelled as a baseball and basketball player for Donora High School. He was supposedly offered a basketball scholarship by the University of Pittsburgh, and Lukasz wanted his son to accept it. Stash, who was not really interested in pursuing his education, wanted to play baseball instead, and, according to him, his mother interceded with tears and persuaded her husband to let their son pursue his dream. In his very fine biography of this baseball great, entitled *Musial,* James N. Giglio calls this story "contrived" in one sentence and "manufactured" in another. He claims that Musial told this story to conceal the fact that Lukasz did not really give in to his wife's wishes and actually stayed angry with his son for several years for choosing a baseball career over a college education. Jim Giglio, has been a close friend of mine for many years and one of Stan Musial's greatest admirers, and I accept his conclusion that the story is not entirely factual.

In spite of the tension that Musial's decision to pursue a professional baseball career might have created in his family, it was no doubt the right decision. Yet, the future baseball great got off to a rocky start. He was 17 years old when he played for Williamson, West Virginia, in the Mountain State League. As a pitcher that first year he won six games and lost six, while as a hitter his batting average was a mediocre .258. His statistics improved during his second season at Williamson. He won nine games and lost two as a pitcher, and his batting average climbed remarkably to .352.

Musial spent most of the 1940 season at Daytona Beach, Florida, where he played for a manager named Dick Kerr. While there his play improved considerably, as he became the top left handed pitcher in the Florida State League. Unfortunately, on August 11, 1940, he sustained an injury while playing centerfield—an injury that ended his career as a pitcher. On the other hand, the injury turned out to be a blessing, since it led to Musial's becoming one of the greatest hitters of all time.

One of the first things everyone noticed about this hitter, who stood six feet tall and weighed 175 pounds, was that he had a unique batting stance. Some called it a "corkscrew stance." Harry Walker, one of Musial's teammates, would observe that no hitter could remain in baseball long with a stance like that. One pitcher described Musial's crouching over home plate as looking like "a kid peeping around the corner to see if the cops were coming." Some said that Musial at the plate looked like a "coiled rattlesnake." No matter what he looked like crouched over home plate, he was destined to make an indelible mark on baseball.

In 1941 Musial started the season in Springfield, Missouri, with a Class C ball club, and joining him there was his wife, Lillian "Lil" Labash, whom he had married the year before in Daytona Beach. Setting up housekeeping in Springfield proved to be short-lived, however. So impressive was Musial's performance as a hitter that he was soon promoted to the Class AA team in Rochester, New York, and on September 17 of that year he made his debut with the St. Louis Cardinals. Going from Class C ball to the major leagues in a single year was a remarkable feat.

The following year, 1942, was Musial's first full year in a Cardinals uniform, and the Cards won the World

Series. In 1943 Musial became the premier player in the National League, if not the majors. He won the National League batting title with a .357 average and led the league in several other batting categories. He was named the league's Most Valuable Player. Then, in 1944, the Cards again won the World Series.

Musial's brilliant career was temporarily interrupted by World War II. In 1945 he enlisted in the U. S. Navy and served for thirteen months, but without seeing combat. After leaving the service he returned to the Cardinals in 1946 and won his second Most Valuable Player award and his third World Series title. Two seasons later, in 1948, he won a third Most Valuable Player award. He finished that season just one home run short of winning the Triple Crown—batting average, runs batted in, and home runs.

For fifteen more seasons "Stan the Man" played in a Cardinals uniform, first as an outfielder and then as a first baseman. His benevolent attitude on the field earned him the friendship and respect that perhaps only a few players ever enjoyed. While some other white players and many fans were harassing Jackie Robinson, the first black player to play in the major leagues, Musial encouraged him. He seemed always to see the best in people. On one occasion, according to one report, an opposing pitcher inadvertently "beaned" Musial, and the great hitter had to be taken to the hospital in an unconscious condition. The pitcher who hit him went to the hospital and anxiously waited outside Musial's room to apologize. Upon regaining consciousness, Musial was told that the pitcher was in distress over the "bean ball" and was waiting to apologize. Musial reportedly told someone in the room to go outside and tell the pitcher not to worry about it, because "I know he didn't mean to do it."

By the time Musial retired in 1963 he held or shared seventeen major league records, twenty-nine National League records, and nine All-Star records. He left baseball with more money and more friends than any other player ever had. On the strength of a career that included a lifetime batting average of .331, 1,951 runs batted in, 3,630 hits, and 475 home runs, he was inducted into the Baseball Hall of Fame in Cooperstown, New York, in 1967, the first year he was eligible. He got 93.2% of the votes on the first ballot. In 1999 he was selected for the Major League Baseball All-Century Team, but an even higher honor awaited him. On February 15, 2011, Musial was awarded the Presidential Medal of Freedom, the highest honor that can be bestowed on a civilian.

In his early career there were few people who foresaw that Musial was destined to be an all-time great, but there was at least one. Charles "Chuck" Schmidt, one of Musial's high school coaches, concluded very early that Stan was "a born natural." When asked what made Musial great, Schmidt answered, "God."

Now for my own encounter with "Stan the Man," my boyhood idol. I rushed up and told Stan who I was and that I was a fan of his. He asked me if I was a Cardinals fan, and I told him I had been one ever since I had known anything about major league baseball. He opened a drawer behind the cash register, pulled out a picture of himself in his Cardinals uniform and asked me if I wanted him to sign it. "Of course, I do," I said. He wrote an inscription and signed it. I told him I had tried to meet him at his restaurant several times and how honored I was to finally do it. I told him that I had some friends at the table who would also like to meet him, if he had time. "Sure," he said. Then he grabbed some more pictures and followed me to the table where we joined several friends who had accompanied me for dinner.

Stan greeted everybody and asked them if they were getting plenty to eat. "I don't want you to leave hungry," he said to everyone. He offered pictures to all and inscribed each picture according to each request. What a gracious and pleasant man. When he left us, we all knew why he had always been so well liked. For me it was a thrilling experience.

I saw Stan Musial one more time after that, but I did not talk to him. I was in St. Louis for a history convention, as I had been several years earlier when I met Stan, and there was a grand social function for the city's celebrities, at our convention hotel. I saw Stan and his wife Lillian passing through the crowd, presumably on their way to the hotel ballroom. Dressed in a tuxedo, Stan looked noticeably older than he had several years before, and his wife, wrapped in what appeared to be an expensive fur coat, looked like a lady well past her prime. Lillian Musial died May 3, 2012. She and Stan had four children, eleven grandchildren, and twelve great grandchildren. The couple had been married for nearly seventy-two years.

One of the most memorable nights of my life was that night in St. Louis when I shook the hand of and spoke to Stan Musial. It would have been an honor, too, to meet Lillian Musial, by all accounts a gracious lady. I didn't have that honor, but I did see her with her husband, and it was obvious that they were a couple devoted to each other—and for just short of seventy-two years! A record! Perhaps not, but certainly rare among celebrities!

Sports heroes come and go, but, as the old saying goes, "They don't make 'em like 'Stan the Man' anymore." At age 92 he remains an American icon.*

*At the time I wrote the words above, Stan Musial was still alive, but now he is gone, having departed this life on January 19, 2013. Our country has lost one its greatest sports heroes.

Dean Rusk

Of the celebrities I have met over the course of my life, my contact with them has been brief and casual with all but three. The three that I came to know fairly well were all great men, and I cherish the memories of interacting with them. One of the three was our country's 53rd secretary of state, Dean Rusk. Mr. Rusk was a speaker on our campus at the University of Montevallo in 1985, and I will recount the story of his coming a little later, including an account of the opportunities that my wife Judy and I had to enjoy his company.

I begin, however, with information about Rusk's distinguished career. In our nation's entire history, only one secretary of state, Cordell Hull, held that office longer than Dean Rusk. The latter's time in the office was eight years (1961-1969), while the former's was eleven years (1933-1944). It is also worth noting that Rusk was one of only two Georgians to occupy the office.

David Dean Rusk began life on February 9, 1909, in Cherokee County, Georgia. He was the son of Robert Hugh Rusk and Frances Elizabeth Clotfelder Rusk. He attended public schools in Atlanta and then took a bachelor's degree at Davidson College in 1931. Although he had to work his way through college, he proved to be an excellent student and was inducted into Phi Beta Kappa, academia's premier honor society. Awarded a Rhodes scholarship, Rusk left Davidson for Oxford University in England, where he earned B. S. and M. A. degrees from St. John's College (1933 and 1934).

During his studies at Oxford there was considerable discussion regarding the proper way to deal with Adolf Hitler and Nazi Germany. The Oxford Union debate society voted overwhelmingly for appeasement, but Rusk demurred. He believed that dictators should not be appeased. Hitler's aggression against various European countries led, of course, to World War II and colored Rusk's attitude toward appeasement for the future. Consequently, while secretary of state during the administration of Lyndon Johnson, Rusk steadfastly advised the president to resist communist forces in Vietnam. Johnson did so and brought about years of American involvement in Southeast Asia to thwart the spread of communism there. Unfortunately, our efforts to achieve that proved to be futile.

Before Rusk arrived at the point where he had an influential voice in American foreign policy, however, he was a college professor. After returning from his days at Oxford, he was a professor of government and later dean of the faculty at Mills College in Oakland, California (1934-1940). While at Mills, Rusk met a student named Virginia Foisie and married her in 1937. The couple became the parents of three children—David, Richard, and Margaret (Peggy) Elizabeth.

Beginning in 1940 there was a long interlude from the classroom for Rusk. He joined the U. S. Army and ultimately ended up in Army Intelligence. By war's end he had attained the rank of colonel and joined the general staff in the War Department in Washington. There he had the opportunity to work with General George C. Marshall. Rusk intended to continue his military career, but in 1947 Marshall, then secretary of state, persuaded him to head the Office of Special Political Affairs (i.e., the U.N. Desk) in the State Department. Both men were opposed to Israel's becoming an independent state and being recognized by the United States, but they acquiesced after President Harry Truman decided in favor of statehood for Israel. As they saw the matter, it was their duty to support the president or resign their offices.

In 1950 Rusk moved up the ladder in the State Department, when Secretary of State Dean Acheson appointed him assistant secretary of state for Far Eastern affairs. His aversion to appeasement surfaced again when he joined Acheson in urging the president to resist communist aggression in Korea.

In the midst of the Korean conflict, 1952, Rusk left government service to become a trustee and later president of the Rockefeller Foundation. His focus in that position was on developing programs for poor nations and highlighting the dangers of nuclear contamination from testing nuclear weapons in the atmosphere.

Returning to government service in 1961, Rusk reached his apogee as a public figure, when President John F. Kennedy appointed him secretary of state. Rumors circulated that Kennedy and Rusk were not on the best of terms and that the president was often critical of his appointee to the highest office in the Cabinet. Even so, Rusk was not reluctant to offer his opinion when critical decisions had to be made. He advised against giving American air support during the Bay of Pigs invasion of Cuba in 1961, and the rag-tag army of Cuban exiles was utterly defeated by the forces of Fidel Castro. Kennedy took heavy flak for the Bay of Pigs fiasco, and, perhaps, he privately blamed that on Rusk.

A better outcome materialized from Rusk's advice the next year during the Cuban Missile crisis. The secretary of state called for a tough diplomatic response to the presence of Russian missiles on Cuban soil, but he opposed the U. S. military's calls for sending forces into Cuba. It was Rusk who proposed the "quarantine" or blockade of Cuba, a strategy that proved successful, because it allowed time for a diplomatic solution to be worked out behind the scenes.

Another Rusk success story was the part he played in bringing about the Nuclear Test Ban Treaty in 1963. He had long opposed nuclear testing in the atmosphere, and his negotiations with the Soviet Union resulted in the agreement by the two super powers to stop the nuclear contamination of the earth's atmosphere. This was a significant development in international diplomacy of which Rusk could be justly proud.

Any popularity that Rusk might have gained from his successes with regard to Cuba and nuclear testing were eventually overshadowed by the situation in Vietnam. American involvement in Vietnam began under President Kennedy, but it was stepped up considerably after Kennedy's assassination by the man who followed him in the Oval Office. Rusk had always been a strong proponent of preventing a communist takeover in the country once known as French Indochina, and his relationship with the new president was much better than it had been with Kennedy. Whether or not Rusk influenced President Johnson in his increasingly aggressive actions in Vietnam is a matter of conjecture, but he undoubtedly supported them. Consequently, America's 53rd secretary of state was vilified on college campuses across the nation, because students condemned our involvement in Southeast Asia by words and, at times, violent demonstrations.

When Richard Nixon ascended to the presidency in 1969, Rusk left his post at the State Department and returned to his native state of Georgia to become a professor of international law at the University of Georgia in Athens. Although Rusk was much admired and respected in that new role, his appointment was denounced by one university trustee because Rusk's daughter had married a black man. In spite of that demonstration of bigotry over his joining the University of Georgia faculty, the former secretary of state continued his association with the university until he died of congestive heart failure on December 20, 1994. He is buried in Oconee Hill Cemetery in Athens.

When it was decided at the University of Montevallo to establish a lecture series for a former heralded faculty member named Hallie Farmer, I was named chairperson of the committee to find our lecturer and told to be sure it was someone with a "big name." Big name! No problem, I thought, at first, because I learned that former President Jimmy Carter's brother-in-law had once taken some classes at the University of Montevallo. For whatever reason, I thought that President Carter would jump at the chance to come to our campus, since he lived only 200 or so miles from us and since his brother-in-law had a connection with us. I was wrong, as it turned out, for the former president immediately turned us down. Our next choice, Madame Anwar Sadat, insisted on a larger speaking fee than we could afford, or at least her agent did. I had met the next celebrity I contacted, and he was a personal friend of fellow faculty member Eugene B. Sledge. Hence, I thought he might surely accept our invitation. Again I was wrong. That celebrity, Studs Terkel, also turned us down. Since we were approaching the time when we planned to hold the lecture series, I began to wonder if we would be forced to kick off the series with someone who was not a "big name."

I don't recall how Dean Rusk's name came up, but when it did I called his office to learn if he might be interested. Time for letters and delayed responses was running out. To my surprise, he answered the telephone, and I had a very pleasant conversation with him. He told me that because of his "advanced age" he was not doing much speaking anymore, but he asked me to send an invitation with details about the proposed lecture series and an explanation of what would be expected of him. He promised to get back to me quickly. When enough time had passed for him to receive the invitation and respond, and when I had heard nothing, I called his office again. His secretary answered and said that she had planned to call me that very day. "Mr. Rusk," she said, "has agreed to accept the invitation."

We had our "big name." I was ecstatic, and we prepared to start the series at the announced time and with as much fanfare as possible. As chairperson of the committee responsible for making the arrangements for the event, it was my duty to escort Mr. Rusk and take care of his needs while he was on our campus. What a great experience that turned out to be. In retrospect, I can honestly say that I was and am glad that the other people we invited turned us down, although I feel sure that spending time with them would also have been personally rewarding. When our distinguished guest was not conducting a lecture, he was with me and sometimes with my wife and me. I came to know him as a brilliant man and one of the truly delightful people it has been my pleasure to know. One of my proudest possessions hangs in my office. It is a picture of Mr. Rusk and me. Above the picture is the copy of an address he delivered May 14, 1965, at Runnymede, England, in celebration of the 750th anniversary of the signing of Magna Carta. The address is a "Memorial to President Kennedy," who was honored that day by having an acre of Runnymede dedicated to the late President. Underneath the copy of the address Mr. Rusk inscribed the words "With deep appreciation to David Morgan" and signed his name under them. That cherished memento will hang on my wall as long as I live.

Students and others who came to hear Rusk deliver the first Hallie Farmer Lectures were enthralled, as he spoke so insightfully about American foreign policy. Besides the formal lectures, he also met with smaller groups of students for question-and-answer sessions, and those were both informative and entertaining. Observing his interaction with students revealed to me why Mr. Rusk had enjoyed so much success as a diplomat. In one of the sessions a student asked him what he thought about incumbent President Ronald Reagan. Mr. Rusk replied, "Mr. Reagan was not my candidate." The room erupted with the applause of students who were Reagan detractors. When it was quiet again, he said, "But he is my president." This time the boisterous applause came from the Reagan supporters. It was clear that our 53rd secretary of state knew how to appeal to people on both sides of an issue.

My favorite memory of my experience with Mr. Rusk involves the occasion when my wife and I took him out for dinner one night. Since I was told to treat him like royalty and ignore the expense, I made reservations to take our guest to our area's best restaurant—a restaurant owned and managed by a friend of mine named Nick Carnes. When I told Mr. Rusk where we were going, he asked if I knew the person who managed the restaurant. I answered, "Yes, he is a close friend of mine." He asked if I would mind calling my friend and asking him not to call any attention to our being there, saying that he wanted to go and have a quiet dinner and remain unnoticed. I told him I would do that. When I called Nick and explained what Mr. Rusk wanted, he said, "Sure, but I can meet him, can't I?" I answered, "Yes, of course you can. Just don't announce his presence."

Nick was excited when we arrived, and he took charge of showing us to our table. Once there, he said quietly—almost in a whisper—"Mr. Rusk, we are honored to have you in our restaurant. We just don't ordinarily have people of your stature to come in."

"Aw," replied the distinguished guest, "I'm just an old country boy from Cherokee County, Georgia. We don't have a restaurant like this in the whole county."

After we ordered our dinner, Mr. Rusk entertained us with several stories. One of them concerned his student days in England. Hitler had recently risen to power in Germany, and Rusk and a fellow student from India went to Berlin out of curiosity. With pride Mr. Rusk told us that his traveling companion had become a lifelong friend and that even then in 1985 they kept in touch regularly. The student from Georgia, along with the student from India, who was of a very dark complexion, decided to attend an outdoor Hitler rally, but they were stopped at the gate. They were told that Rusk could enter, but the other student could not, because only "Aryans" were allowed to attend. Rusk proceeded to challenge the Storm Trooper who attended the gate, telling him that his friend was from India and that he was one of the purest Aryans on earth. Probably thinking that only Nordics were Aryans the gate attendant was confused, and he called for his superior. Reluctantly, the superior who knew a little more history than the underling, had to agree with Rusk and let them both enter.

Another story told by Mr. Rusk that night, my favorite, concerned Soviet Foreign Minister Andrei Gromyko. Before he began the story, Rusk asked, "David, is Judy a big girl?" I answered affirmatively, wondering why he asked. He sensed that I was curious about the question and said, "Some might think I shouldn't tell what I am about to tell in mixed company." I assured him that it would be fine and told him to go ahead.

He proceeded, noting that over the course of several years as their respective countries' top diplomats, he and Gromyko had become friends. The foreign minister came to the United States to have discussions with Rusk about some negotiations that had stalled. Before announcing the presence of someone as important as Gromyko and before beginning the negotiations, it was customary to call a press conference. Prior to appearing before the press, the two men and their aides discussed what they would say in their opening statements. They agreed that they wanted to announce that they would have intimate talks about American-Soviet differences on foreign policy matters, and they even discussed what figures of speech they might use:

"shoulder to shoulder," "face to face," "eyeball to eyeball," etc. When Gromyko told his translator that he would deliver his opening statement in English, the translator objected strenuously, assuring the foreign minister that doing so was contrary to protocol. Of course, he didn't dare tell Gromyko, but must have thought, "Besides, sir, your command of English stinks." Gromyko overruled the translator.

Rusk addressed the press corps by indicating that he and his Russian counterpart were going to have frank discussion, man to man, face to face. After Rusk finished, Gromyko stood before the reporters and said that he was happy to be in Washington with his friend, Dean Rusk, and that they were going to talk "balls to balls."

Over a quarter of a century has passed since that delightful night Judy and I spent with Mr. Rusk. I remember it as if it were a few days ago, and I cherish every remembrance of it. I wish I could remember the lectures this great man gave as well as I remember our personal times together, but I cannot. I can truly say that I never spent time with anyone other than family and old friends who was more delightful to be around. I recall hearing about Mr. Rusk's death in 1994, and I was deeply saddened by the news. He was a rare man and a great American.

Kenny Rogers

Unlike my experience with Dean Rusk, I did not get to know Kenny Rogers, arguably one of the greatest crossover pop/country singers of my generation. I saw him twice and spoke face to face with him only once. The details of that encounter will appear below, but first a bit of the Kenny Rogers story.

Kenneth Donald Rogers was born in Houston, Texas, on August 21, 1938. He was one of seven children born to a father who was a carpenter and a mother who was a nurse. The family was poor and had to make their residence in a federal housing project. That was destined to change when Kenny climbed to fame and fortune in the music business.

His career began in the 1950s, and for a time he bounced around from one group to another. First he was with The Scholars and next The Bobby Doyle Trio. Then he worked with Mickey Gilley and Eddy Arnold before joining The New Christy Minstrels as a singer and double bass player in 1966. Hardly a year had passed with that group before he and several members broke away and formed The First Edition in 1967. With this group Kenny hit it big on two singles—"Ruby, Don't Take Your Love to Town" and "Reuben James." Other hits followed, and Kenny was on his way to the big time. For a while he had a hippie image with his long hair, an ear ring, and pink sunglasses.

Though still popular, The First Edition split up in 1976, and Rogers launched his solo career. He recorded numerous hits, none bigger than "Lucille," in 1977. It was number one in five countries and sold over five million records. Because of that song, his album *Kenny Rogers* made it to number one on the Billboard Country Album

Chart. Following that album there was another multi-million seller called *The Gambler* and another international number one single called "The Coward of the County."

In the middle of his fabulous solo career Rogers branched out and began singing duets with popular female solo artists. He had monumental duet hits with Dottie West ("Every Time Two Fools Collide"), Kim Carnes ("Don't Fall in Love with a Dreamer"), and Dolly Parton ("Islands in the Stream'). He teamed up with other great names in the music business, too—Lionel Richie, Ronnie Milsap, The Bee Gees, and others.

At age 62 in 2000 he had another spectacular number one single called "Buy Me a Rose." At that time he became the oldest artist to have a number one hit, but two years later Willie Nelson at age 70 took that distinction away from Rogers when he teamed up with Toby Keith to sing "Beer for My Horses." By 2011 Kenny had recorded 65 albums and had sold 190 million records.

His fabulous singing career opened the door for a movie career as well. A movie based on his hit single and known as *The Gambler* provided him a brief career in film. He also ventured into some uncharted waters when he decided to go into the food business. He launched a restaurant chain known as Kenny Rogers Roasters. My wife and I ate at one of the restaurants from time to time and found the food delicious. I for one am sorry that his venture into the food business ultimately failed.

Rogers also had failures in his private life. He has been married five times and has five children. So far his longest lasting marriage was to Marianne Gordon, a member of the cast on the popular television show *Hee Haw*. They were married from 1977 to 1993 and had one child. He has been married to his fifth wife, Wanda Miller, since June 1, 1997. She gave birth to his twin sons, Jordan and Justin, on his 66th birthday, August 21, 2003.

By all accounts Kenny Rogers has had one of the most remarkable careers in music of any singer ever. In 1986 he was voted "Favorite Singer of All-Time!" He has received countless music awards, including several highly prestigious Grammy awards. And he is still performing at age 74.

Back in the 1980s, I saw Kenny Rogers twice and spoke to him once. I don't remember the exact year. I happened to be in Athens, Georgia, where the NCAA tennis finals were being played at the University of Georgia tennis complex. An added feature to that event was some exhibition doubles in which several celebrities played. One of the celebrities was Kenny Rogers, and another was Hank Aaron, one of baseball's all-time great home run hitters. Aaron was the first to break Babe Ruth's home run record of 714 in a career. Also playing in the exhibition match that I saw was Gardnar "Gar" Mulloy, who was the only tennis celebrity playing in the exhibition match. Mulloy, probably around 70 at the time, had won the Wimbledon men's doubles title at age 43 in 1957 with his partner, Budge Patty, who was 33. With another partner, Bill Talbert, Mulloy won four U. S. men's doubles titles. He was inducted into the International Tennis Hall of Fame in 1972. I can't recall the name of the fourth player who participated in the match. I would have been honored to speak to any of the three whose names are mentioned above, but there was no opportunity to do so.

The next day, however, I returned to the tennis center and happened to see Kenny Rogers walking out. He had just played with someone, and he was on his way home to his rather elaborate mansion and estate just outside of Athens. I happened to have some paper and a pen, and so I rushed up to Rogers and told him that I was a fan of his. He was very pleasant in greeting me. I asked if he would give me an autograph, because if my wife knew I talked to him and didn't get an autograph that "she would kill me."

Rogers quickly said, "Give me a pen. I don't want that on my conscience." I laughed, he signed his name on the paper I had handed him and told me that he had to head home, since he was already later than the time Marianne was expecting him

Kenny Rogers went on his way, and I stood where I was for a moment thinking how envious Judy was going to be when I got back to Montevallo and how thrilled I was to have actually met and gotten the autograph of one of my favorite singers. More than two decades after that encounter he is still one of my favorite singers. It was both a pleasure and an honor to meet "The Gambler."

Junius Scales

My next celebrity became a celebrity for notoriety more than for widespread popularity. Indeed, he was very unpopular with many of his fellow North Carolinians and many Americans who knew who he was. Although he was born into a very prestigious and well off family, as a young man he felt the pain of black and poor white people and decided that the only way to change their degraded lives was to work for a communist America. Ultimately, that resulted in his becoming the first person in the United States to go to prison for a violation of the Smith Act of 1940. He was accused of belonging to an organization "suspected" of plotting the overthrow of the United States government. I met him more than thirty years after his arrest in 1954, and my encounter with him was brief. Even so, because of all I had heard about Junius Scales, the man I met was definitely not the man I expected to meet when we were introduced. I will describe the meeting later, but first I offer a sketch of Scales' unusual life.

Junius Irving Scales was born in Greensboro, North Carolina, on March 26, 1920, into a socially prominent family, as was already noted. He had a great uncle, A. M. Scales, who had been governor of the state. Scales was obviously very bright, as he matriculated at the University of North Carolina when he was only 16 years old. Before that he had worked at The Intimate Bookshop in Chapel Hill, a hangout for the avant-garde of the academic community. Perhaps radical would be a more accurate word than avant-garde, since the owner of the shop ran a communist printing operation in the back room. During his student days, Scales, on his 19th birthday, joined the Communist Party.

Soon after embracing communism, Scales married his first wife, Vera, quit school, and became a union organizer in the textile mills of North Carolina. His labor activism was interrupted by the Japanese attack on Pearl Harbor, after which he volunteered for military service and spent the years 1942-1946 in the U. S. Army.

After being discharged from the Army in 1946, Scales returned to Chapel Hill and re-entered the university. He received his bachelor's degree and then began work on his master's, all the while serving as local Communist Party organizer. He held meetings in his home that were open to party members and outsiders as well. In 1948 he became state party chairman in North Carolina and openly identified himself as such. Newspaper stories about him proved increasingly embarrassing to his prominent, wealthy family and produced a strain on his marriage that finally led to divorce.

Scales did not remain single for long. In 1950 he married his second wife, Gladys, who was a New Yorker. A daughter, Barbara, was born to the couple in Durham, North Carolina, the next year. By the time his daughter was born in 1951, Junius Scales was traveling from city to city under assumed names, organizing the Communist Party in North Carolina, South Carolina, Tennessee, Virginia, and Mississippi. He held secret meetings in the homes of party members to recruit members, collect dues, and promote the party's fortunes. Because he was so often gone from home, his wife and daughter moved back to New York City. He visited them at intervals.

As Scales traveled about conducting the business of the Communist Party, he was followed and observed by the FBI. By 1954 the authorities were convinced they had enough evidence to arrest and convict him, and he was taken into custody in Memphis, Tennessee. Indicted under a provision of the Smith Act as a member of an organization advocating the violent overthrow of the U. S.

government, he was destined to become the only member of the Communist Party to serve time in prison on that charge.

After his conviction, Scales remained free on bail while his appeal made its way through the federal courts. His case, *Scales v. United States,* dragged on during one appeal after another for seven years. In 1961 the case was heard by the United States Supreme Court, which decided against Scales in a 5 to 4 decision. Sentenced to six years, he began serving his time in October 1961.

Meanwhile, Scales had abandoned his allegiance to the Communist Party. He had served as party chairman in North Carolina until 1956, when he became disenchanted with communism because of the Soviet Union's invasion of Hungary. Then, in 1957, he quit the Communist Party altogether, when Nikita Khrushchev revealed atrocities that had been committed by Joseph Stalin during the days of Stalin's communist dictatorship. Years later Scales would reflect on his days as a communist in a memoir entitled *Cause at Heart: A Former Communist Remembers*, which he wrote with Richard Nickson. Looking back, he said, "Stalin, my revered symbol of the infallibility of Communism, the builder of socialism in one country, the rock of Stalingrad, the wise, kindly man with the keen sense of humor at whose death I had wept just three years before—Stalin had been a murderous, power-hungry monster." He added, "My idol had crumbled to dust forever."

For his attachment to Stalin and communism, Scales had spent time in the federal penitentiary at Lewisburg, Pennsylvania—not the six years to which he had been sentenced but fifteen months, because President John F. Kennedy commuted his sentence. A number of prominent people importuned Kennedy on Scales' behalf. Among them were Socialist Party leader Norman Thomas, civil rights leader Martin Luther King, theologian Reinhold

Niebuhr, and literary luminary W. H. Auden. In making his appeal to the president on behalf of Scales, Niebuhr referred to the former communist as "a misguided ideologue," and added, "There is something un-American in having even one political prisoner in the United States." The voices of such influential people, along with others, persuaded the president to grant the commutation, and Scales walked away from Lewisburg a free man on Christmas Eve, 1962.

After being released from prison Scales moved to Pine Bush, New York, and worked as a proofreader for the *New York Times*. He lived for the remainder of his life in New York, dying at Mt. Sinai Hospital in Manhattan on August 5, 2002.

Over many years as a resident and student in North Carolina, I had heard of Junius Scales, but I never dreamed I would ever meet him. It was by accident that I did. At the 1996 annual meeting of the Southern Historical Association in Little Rock, Arkansas, I left the convention hotel one morning with some friends to eat at an off-site restaurant. Upon entering the restaurant I spotted a fellow historian whom I had seen over the years at the annual SHA meetings. We were not close friends, but we were born in adjoining North Carolina counties (he in Robeson and I in Cumberland), and we had both taken our graduate degrees at the University of North Carolina in Chapel Hill. He was William McKee Evans, professor of history at California State Polytechnic University, Pomona. The only time Bill Evans and I ever saw each other was at SHA annual meetings, and we never did more than carry on casual conversations and exchange pleasantries.

On the occasion of seeing him at the restaurant in Little Rock, I noticed that he was accompanied by a distinguished looking man, presumably a friend. I walked over to greet Bill. We shook hands, asked each other how the other was doing, and he said, "David, meet my friend

Junius Scales. You have probably heard of him." I was taken aback, and said something like, "I believe I have. Do you mean this is *the* Junius Scales?" Mr. Scales laughed and said he was indeed. I wasn't sure what to say next, and I finally said, "I believe we have in common that both of us spent some time in Chapel Hill." He asked me when I was there, and I told him 1962-1964. He laughed again and said, "I had been in jail several times by then." I replied that I had heard that about him. We talked for another minute or two about what I can no longer remember, and then I told him and Bill Evans that I had better join my friends who had been seated at a table. I told Junius Scales that it had been my pleasure to meet him, and I told Bill Evans that it was good to see him again, and the SHA annual meeting wouldn't be the same if our paths didn't cross during it.

Although I am upholding Junius Scales as the celebrity that I met that day, William McKee Evans was something of a celebrity in his own right. A fine historian, Bill has written some excellent books that have contributed to the historical literature in his field, including *Open Wound: The Long View of Race in America; Ballots and Fence Rails;* and *To Die Game: The Story of the Lowry Band, Indian Guerrillas of Reconstruction.* The last book mentioned is about Henry Berry Lowry, a Lumbee Indian, who holds the distinction of being the most notorious outlaw in North Carolina history. In 1872 Lowry, after creating considerable turmoil in eastern North Carolina, dropped out of sight, and to this day nobody knows what happened to him. Like Evans, Lowry was a native of Robeson County. Evans ranks as one of the foremost historians of the Reconstruction era in North Carolina history.

When I encountered Bill Evans and Junius Scales that day in Little Rock, I had no idea, of course, that sixteen years later I would be writing about meeting them. I always had a high regard for Evans, and I must say that Junius Scales made a favorable impression on me, even if he had once been, as Reinhold Niebuhr called him, "a misguided ideologue." After meeting the man, I have to believe that he was probably sincere in trying to be a champion of the downtrodden in our society. I don't applaud him for choosing communism to achieve that, but I do think his motives sprang from a good heart, and I am glad my path crossed his.

Eugene B. ("Sledgehammer") Sledge

Gene Sledge and I were faculty colleagues for nearly twenty years, and I knew him for nearly ten years longer than that. When I moved with my wife and two children to Montevallo, Alabama, in August of 1973, the Sledges were among the first people we met. Gene and his wife Jeanne had two sons, John and Henry. My son Brian, who was seven at that time, needed to find a playmate, and a mutual friend put us in touch with the Sledges, who didn't live very far from our new residence. Brian and Henry quickly became friends and played together quite a bit, and I soon enjoyed the company of Henry's father as a fellow faculty member, despite the fact that we were in different disciplines and our buildings were across the campus from each other. I had never heard of Gene Sledge before. He was not assertive and was a generally congenial man. He could be as humble as a monk or as direct as his Marine drill instructor must have been. It didn't take long before I realized that he was a man of conviction. He believed what he believed, and he didn't mind telling you what that was. At that point in his life, nobody had even a hint, and especially not Gene himself, that he was destined to become a celebrity by writing one of the greatest war memoirs ever written. I will tell that story below, but first I will give some biographical information about this man whom I feel so fortunate to have known personally. Even more, I am proud we called each other friend.

Eugene Bondourant Sledge was born November 4, 1923, in Mobile, Alabama. He died March 3, 2001, in Montevallo, Alabama. From his childhood on he loved to read. He was a frail child, but his physician father wouldn't let him live a sheltered life. He took his son hunting and fishing at an early age. Consequently, Gene learned to love the outdoors and the woods.

He was among the graduates of Murphy High School in Mobile in 1942, and in the fall of that year he entered Marion Military Institute. However, the bombing of Pearl Harbor the previous year kept weighing on his mind, and he didn't remain at Marion long. Feeling the urge to serve his country, he enlisted in the U. S. Marine Corps on December 3, 1942. Eventually, he was assigned to K Company, 3rd Battalion, 5th Marines, 1st Marine Division. He achieved the rank of private first class in the Pacific Theater. He saw action as a 60mm mortar man in the Peleliu and Okinawa campaigns. He also saw action as a stretcher bearer and rifleman.

Sledge entered fierce combat for the first time on the island of Peleliu in September 1944. Six months later his unit went into combat again on Okinawa. That battle lasted three months and was one of the costliest of the Pacific war. Fifty thousand soldiers, sailors, and Marines were killed, wounded, or declared missing in action. Young Private Sledge, nicknamed "Sledgehammer" by his fellow Marines, saw 82 days of combat on Okinawa. He survived the battle without a scar, but he was scarred for life by the psychological aftereffects of it. Not long before he died, he said to me, "Don't encourage anybody to contact me about their war, because I'm still trying to get over my war."

Throughout his days of bitter combat in the Pacific, Gene kept notes of what was happening all around him, and those notes became the basis for his highly acclaimed war memoir entitled *With the Old Breed at Peleliu and Okinawa*. When the fighting ended he was sent to Beijing (called Peking at that time), China, for a brief time, and that is where he ended his active duty. In February 1946, he was discharged from the Marines with the rank of corporal.

Upon returning to Alabama, Gene matriculated at Auburn University, where he was awarded his bachelor's degree in 1949. After graduation he decided to try his hand at the insurance and real estate business in Mobile. In 1952 he married Jeanne Arceneaux of that city. Their first son, John, was born in 1957, and their second son, Henry, in 1965. In the meantime, Gene continued his education, earning a master's degree from Auburn. He wrote his master's thesis on parasitic worms—the effects of nematodes on corn. Next, he took his doctorate in zoology from the University of Florida in 1960. For two years after receiving his doctoral degree he worked for the Florida State Department of Agriculture before joining the biology faculty of what was then Alabama College and is now the University of Montevallo. From 1962 to 1991 he taught introductory biology, physiology, and the history and philosophy of science. During the 18 or 19 years that Gene and I taught together, I heard many a student moaning about Dr. Sledge being such a tough teacher. It became quite clear to me that students had to learn his material or suffer the consequences for not doing so.

And now for some personal stories about the man who was sometimes gentle and sometimes gruff. I begin by proudly saying that Gene and I never said a cross word to each other. I never asked a favor of him that he didn't grant. On one occasion I asked him if he would speak to my history seminar about his famous book, and, as I recall, it was after he had retired from teaching. The seminar met at night, an inconvenient time for him, but he came, and the students were awe-struck by what he had to say. He always spoke from his heart and soul, and he always answered every question I ever heard put to him honestly and directly.

Gene was never a man who sought attention, and he grew weary of invitations to speak at this or that conference. I got a call one day from a friend and fellow historian at the University of Alabama. He was in charge of putting together an annual conference on military history, a rather prestigious meeting in the state. My friend had attempted unsuccessfully to get in touch with Gene to invite him to participate in the conference as one of the speakers. "David," he said, "I can't get Dr. Sledge to respond to my letters or return my calls. Do you know him well?" I answered that I did, and he asked if I would intercede for him and tell Dr. Sledge that he was a reputable historian and ask him to respond, "If you think that," he added. I told him I would make the call, but that I could not guarantee positive results. I knew how Gene had come to feel about invitations to speak, and I knew too that he was an Auburn man and did not have a high regard for the University of Alabama—something I did not mention to my friend.

When I called Gene and told him about my friend's request, he was not thrilled with the prospect of speaking at another conference, and, as I had anticipated, especially not one in Tuscaloosa. I explained to him that my friend over at the University of Alabama was a fine historian and a good man who was just trying to put together an outstanding conference on military history and thought Gene would make a great presenter. He told me that he had grown weary of conferences but that he would think it over and get back to my friend with an answer one way or the other. I don't remember what happened following my conversation with Gene, and I don't know now whether he participated or not. Yet, I have every confidence that he did what he told me he would do. He didn't make empty promises.

Another story about this man concerns birds and cats. Gene was passionate about birds, and he hated cats because they preyed on birds. One of our colleagues at the University of Montevallo was a woman in the Music Department. She was a cat lover, and had several cats, cats that she did not keep at home. Her home was across the street and a few doors down from the Sledges. When Gene saw her cats stalking "my birds" in his yard, he called the woman and told her to keep her cats at home. She said that she could not always keep her cats indoors, because they needed exercise. I heard from various sources that Gene told her in no uncertain terms that he had better not see them in his yard again. He ended up appealing to the city to make animal owners keep their animals at home, and he threatened to make some anti-freeze available to our colleague's cats if she or the city continued to let them roam. Cats, I have been told, love anti-freeze, but, of course, drinking it kills them.

There was much talk in town about the cat controversy on Cardinal Crest Drive, but it eventually passed. I heard that the lady was informed by the city that Montevallo had been a bird sanctuary since the 1930s and that she had to keep her cats at home or Animal Control would pick them up. She solved the problem by building a house and moving south of town to a different county where her cats could stalk and prey upon birds with impunity.

One of my memories of Gene has to do with an event at which I was the speaker. Montevallo is privileged to have within its city limits a remarkable place called The American Village. It is a place established to commemorate and promote an understanding of America's heritage. Its founder is Tom Walker, a graduate of the University of Montevallo, who is currently a member of the school's board of trustees. Though not as well-known or as prestigious as Williamsburg, Virginia or Sturbridge Village, Massachusetts, The American Village has acquired quite a reputation in its twelve years of existence. Jim Rees, who is director of Mount Vernon, has visited Montevallo twice, and he told me that the presence of The American Village has given Montevallo and Alabama a prominent place among historical places of its kind nationally. On the occasion in question, I spoke at the village about my book entitled *The Devious Dr. Franklin, Colonial Agent: Benjamin Franklin's Years in London.* Gene attended my presentation, along with his wife Jeanne. He had purchased a copy of my book and asked me to autograph it and inscribe it to him and his wife. I was more than happy to do that, but I spelled his wife's name with one "n" instead of two, not knowing that she spelled it that way. When an opportunity presented itself, Gene approached me with the book and asked, "David, would you mind changing the spelling of Jeanne's name? It has two 'ns' in it." I was more than glad to do it, but was embarrassed that I had known Jeanne for so many years and didn't know how to spell her name correctly. Two things struck me about that incident. First, Gene approached me with a shyness I had never seen in him before, almost like a little boy asking for a big favor. Second, Gene called me David. Most the time he called me Dave or Davidius. He is the only person who has ever called me Davidius. I suppose he did it out of his affinity for classical literature. What I would give, if I could hear him call me that again!

I am almost embarrassed to tell another story about Gene, because it demonstrates that I am not a person of much foresight. One of our campus committees was called the Research and Special Projects Committee. I was chairperson of that committee for a number of years. One day Gene talked to me about securing a grant from the committee to help him financially with typing his manuscript about his experiences in the Pacific theater during World War II. I told him that the committee was supposed to support proposals for people doing research or writing in their fields and that this proposal didn't appear to do that. He replied that he was aware of that but said that he would appreciate it if I would present it to the committee anyway. He asked for just a few hundred dollars, if I remember correctly. I told him I would move it forward, but I could not promise that he would get anything. As I recall, the committee was somewhat skeptical of the proposal but was willing to go along with it, if the president of the university approved. When I took it to the president, I reminded him that the proposal had nothing to do with Gene's field and thought he might think it necessary to reject it. Instead, he was willing to make an exception to the rule, he said, if the committee was all right with it. After we discussed whether or not it would set a bad precedent and undermine the purpose of the Research and Special Projects program, the president encouraged me to approve the grant and said he would sign off on it.

In retrospect, I wonder how I could ever have been skeptical of the proposal. Gene asked for only a little money to help with typing his manuscript and preparing it for publication. Out of the small sum that was granted-- following considerable questioning—came the second most famous book ever written in Alabama (Harper Lee's *To Kill a Mockingbird* is the most famous.) and, more importantly, one of the top ten books ever written on military history—not American military history, world military history! Some have heralded it as the most important war memoir ever written. It is a book mentioned in the same breath with *The History of the Peloponnesian War* by Thucydides, *We Were Soldiers Once and Young* by Lt. General Harold G. Moore and Joseph L. Galloway, and *All Quiet on the Western Front* by Erich Maria Remarque. And I had doubts about the project? What was I thinking? My only defense is that I was being a legalist who was trying to abide strictly by our committee's criteria for all submitted proposals. And, yet, if we had not opted for some flexibility in this case, a highly significant book might not have seen the light of day, or at least would have been delayed in its publication.

Gene's book, *With the Old Breed at Peleliu and Okinawa,* brought much glory and honor to the campus of the University of Montevallo. Some of the nation's premier historians and writers came to Montevallo because of it. Although Studs Terkel didn't speak on our campus, he did interview Gene and came to visit him. Because of Gene, I met Terkel, and I will tell that story when I discuss the famous Chicagoan. Two who did speak on our campus were Paul Fussel and Stephen Ambrose. Fussel, known for his great book entitled *The Great War and Modern Memory*, was an academician who spent the last few years of his teaching career at the University of Pennsylvania. I was not involved in bringing him to our campus, but I did hear him speak. I just remember that he made glowing remarks about Gene's book.

It was different with Stephen Ambrose, who came to our campus as a Hallie Farmer lecturer. I was chairperson of the committee that invited him. Ambrose's writings were extensive and wide ranging. He had written a great deal of military history, most notably *Band of Brothers* and *D-Day,* and at that time he was president of the National World War II Museum in New Orleans, Louisiana. His work had been praised by many and condemned by a few. His critics charged him with plagiarism and being guilty of factual errors. At the time he came to Montevallo, he had recently written *Undaunted Courage*, which is a historical account of the Lewis and Clark expedition. The book drew almost universal praise, and Ambrose focused on it in the lecture series. I introduced him at the first lecture, and Gene Sledge introduced him at one of the subsequent lectures. Gene took the opportunity to tell the audience a story about one of his lighter moments during the horrors of his time in the Pacific, and then he praised Ambrose and thanked him for coming to our campus. Ambrose was visibly moved by being introduced by our local hero. At the podium he gathered himself, and said, "I have never been more honored in my life than I have been by being introduced by E. B. Sledge." That statement indicated to me that Gene Sledge has made a mark on the writing of military history that will last as long as civilization endures.

In March of 2001 I attended Gene's funeral at the Montevallo Methodist Church. The U. S. Marine Corps sent two colonels and an honor guard to participate at the event. One of the colonels, Joseph Alexander, a noted writer on naval history, gave the eulogy for Gene, one of the most moving and eloquent declarations that I have ever heard. What I would give for a written copy of it! I tried to secure one by asking Jeanne Sledge, Gene's widow, to ask Colonel Alexander for a copy. He responded by saying that he spoke from notes and not a script and could not provide a written copy. What a pity! It is a loss to the world that his eulogy does not exist on paper. I spoke to Colonel Alexander after the funeral, told him that I was a longtime friend of Gene's, and praised the colonel for the outstanding eulogy he had delivered. He thanked me for the kind words about his eulogy, and then he said, "Thank you for being his friend." I thought to myself, "Colonel, being Gene Sledge's friend was my honor."

I will never forget Gene Sledge. I knew him for years, and I never knew what a great man he was. I guess I didn't know because he didn't know. Even when he became famous and saw his war memoir lauded by very important people, he remained the same down-to-earth man and colleague that I had long known. If he ever knew what a great thing he had done by writing *With the Old Breed at Peleliu and Okinawa,* he never flaunted that achievement.

Rest in peace, "Sledgehammer."

Eugene Clifton Stallings, Jr.

Coach Gene Stallings was born in Paris, Texas, March 2, 1935. He attended the Paris public schools and played end on the Paris High School football team. On the team with him was the future National Football League star, Raymond Berry, who caught passes thrown by the legendary quarterback, Johnny Unitas. Stallings was recruited to play football at Texas A&M University by Coach Raymond George, but George was replaced by Coach Paul "Bear" Bryant. Determined to toughen up his team, Bryant took his team to Junction, Texas, for what amounted to a football boot camp in oppressive summer heat. Stallings was one of the famed "Junction Boys." In 1956 he helped lead A&M to its first Southwestern conference championship since 1939.

In 1957 Stallings finished his studies and took his B.S. degree at A&M. By 1958 Coach Bryant had moved on to the University of Alabama and Stallings joined his coaching staff as a defensive assistant. While Stallings was on Bryant's staff, Alabama won two national championships—1961 and 1964.

Meanwhile, Stallings married Ruth Ann Jack, and the couple had five children, four daughters and one son, John Mark, known to the family as Johnny and to whom the coach was devoted. Johnny was born with Down Syndrome, prompting his father to work diligently for the developmentally disabled.

When A&M went in search of a new head football coach in 1965, the school turned to one of their own and brought Stallings home. During a tenure that spanned seven years at that position, Stallings had a pathetic record—27 wins, 45 losses, and 1 tie. His only significant moment during his years at A&M was winning the Southwestern Conference title in 1967 and defeating Coach

Bear Bryant's Alabama team in the Cotton Bowl on January 1, 1968.

From coaching at A&M Stallings went on to the National Football League, coaching the defensive backs for the Dallas Cowboys for a number of years. While he was at that position, the Cowboys won the Super Bowl. In 1986 he became head coach of the St. Louis Cardinals and remained in that position for a short time after the Cardinals moved to Phoenix, Arizona. Near the end of the 1989 season he was removed from his position by the general manager of the Cardinals, Larry Wilson. His record during his years with the Cardinals was an anemic 23 wins, 34 losses, and 1 tie.

Returning to college football after a disappointing career as a head coach in the NFL, Stallings became head coach at the University of Alabama in 1990. There he had started his coaching career, and there he finally enjoyed some real success. His first team went 7-5, and in 1991 it went 11-1 and defeated Colorado in the Blockbuster Bowl. Stallings achieved ultimate success in 1992 by going undefeated, winning the Southeastern Conference Championship, defeating Miami in the Sugar Bowl, and securing the national championship on the strength of 13 wins and no losses.

Alabama continued to win in 1993, 1994, and 1995, but an NCAA investigation led to Alabama's being charged with four major violations of NCAA rules. Stallings was implicated along with Athletic Director Hootie Ingram. The school was disciplined by being placed on probation for three years and by being forced to give up thirty football scholarships. Eight games won and one tie were taken away for the 1993 season, leaving Alabama with 1 win and 12 losses for the year. Moreover, Alabama was barred from post season competition for 1995. In spite of the penalties imposed by the NCAA, Alabama bounced back and had winning seasons in 1994, 1995, and 1996.

The team capped off its winning season in 1996 by winning 17-14 over Michigan in the Outback Bowl. Stallings' record at the time of his retirement in 1997 was 62 wins and 25 losses, but 70 wins, 16 losses, and 1 tie if the forfeited games of the 1993 season are not counted.

Even though Stallings' coaching career consisted of many ups and downs, many honors have come his way. He was Southeastern Conference coach of the year in 1992 and 1994. He has been inducted into the Alabama Sports Hall of Fame, the Texas Sports Hall of Fame, the Texas A&M Hall of Fame, the Cotton Bowl Hall of Fame, and, in 2010 the College Football Hall of Fame.

Off the field, Gene Stallings has earned acclaim as a humanitarian. Because of his efforts on behalf of people with disabilities, a school for children with disabilities is named for him at the University of Alabama, and the playground at that school is called the John Mark Stallings Playground. John Mark, who died of a congenital heart defect on August 2, 2008, was the only individual to appear in two nationally shown United Way commercials. "Johnny's" death touched the hearts of many. Bob Riley, the governor of Alabama in 2008, sent an Alabama state trooper, to Paris, Texas, to lead John Mark Stallings' funeral procession, and Faulkner University in Montgomery, Alabama, named its football field after him and unveiled a statue of him there on October 5, 2012. John Mark lives on in many hearts, and at the time of this writing, his father continues to be a notable humanitarian. Currently, he is building a hospital for the poor of Haiti.

After leaving coaching behind, Stallings moved back to Paris, Texas, and became a cattle rancher, calling his ranch by the name of Hike-A-Way Ranch. He lived there with his wife and son. As long as John Mark lived he was, as was his father, a devoted fan of the Alabama Crimson Tide. On one notable occasion, Stallings asked his son who his favorite college football team was, and, as expected, John Mark said, "The Crimson Tide." Then Stallings asked his son, "Who is your favorite coach?" When John Mark answered with Nick Saban, Stallings asked him, "What about your poor old daddy?" To that John Mark replied, "But you are not there anymore."

I never knew John Mark Stallings, and I know that has to be my loss. And I never really knew Coach Stallings, but I did meet him. The coach and I were on the Texas A&M campus together for a couple of years (1968 and 1969), but our paths never crossed. I attended some of the home games of the team without ever seeing Stallings, except for watching him walk the sidelines from my seat in the stands. It was long after both of us left A&M that I finally met him. Although Stallings never became the celebrity in Alabama that Bear Bryant was, he became quite well known across the length and breadth of the state. Most Alabamians knew him on sight. He was seen on many television commercials, and he still is. Even in late 2012 he appears often in commercials, particularly for the Carl Cannon Automobile Dealership in Jasper, Alabama. Consequently, my wife Judy and I had no trouble spotting him walking by himself to catch an airline flight in the Dallas/Fort Worth Airport.

"That's Coach Stallings right over there," I told Judy. She agreed, and I said, "Let's go over and speak to him." We did, and he stuck out his hand and greeted us. He was very friendly, thanking us for recognizing him and speaking to him. It was March of 2009, and John Mark had just died seven months earlier, and so Judy began by telling him how sorry we were to hear about his son's passing away. He thanked us and said, "Yes, Johnny was a great one." We proceeded to walk with the coach and talk about Alabama. He was involved in the conversation and paid no attention to where we were in the terminal. Finally, I asked what his gate number was. When he answered, I said, "Coach, we passed that gate a little ways back." He replied,

"That's what happens when you are having a good conversation. You forget about what you are doing."

The coach shook our hands, told us he was glad to have met us, and turned to walk back to his gate. We, of course, told him how good it was to meet and talk to him and said goodbye. I have been told many stories about what a rough and rugged man Gene Stallings is, but that was not my impression. Perhaps he takes on a different persona when he does his business as a coach, but as a man we found him congenial and almost humble. My wife and I are proud to have met him and to have enjoyed his company for probably ten or fifteen minutes. It would be my pleasure to talk to him and know him better, if I am ever fortunate enough to encounter him again.

Louis "Studs" Terkel

Studs Terkel was a name I had heard. His book entitled *The Good War: An Oral History of World War II* was highly acclaimed and won for him the Pulitzer Prize in 1985. Since my main interest in American history was in a much earlier period, it was not a book that captured my interest. I never dreamed that Terkel's interest in World War II would bring him to Montevallo, Alabama, and that I would meet him, but that did happen. It happened because of Gene Sledge's famous book, about which I have already said much. As already noted, Terkel came to Montevallo to meet and interview Gene.

The Sledges had a reception for Terkel at their home and invited some friends. Judy and I were fortunate enough to be invited, and I was fortunate enough to have a one-on-one conversation with Terkel. At that juncture, he was already famous for a multitude of achievements, but he did not talk to me about himself or his achievements. He talked to me about Gene and Gene's book. I don't remember much about our conversation, but I vividly recall his praise for *With the Old Breed at Peleliu and Okinawa.* He called it a great anti-war book and said he did not see how anyone could read that book and not hate war. During our conversation Terkel impressed me as a man who loved and respected humanity, a man who would never look down his nose at any fellow human being. If I had to describe him in a few words, he was a man who was respectful of others and their opinions while remaining quietly committed to his own views.

Of all the people I have met in my life, Terkel probably had the most varied and interesting career. He worked for the government, hosted a radio show, hosted a television show, was an actor who played on stage and screen, and a writer who was engaged in a number of literary pursuits. His extraordinary life spanned 96 years.

Louis Terkel was born May 16, 1912, in New York City. He was the youngest of three sons born to Samuel Terkel, a Russian Jewish immigrant who was a tailor by trade, and to Anna Finkel, a Polish woman with an attitude, according to her youngest son—"What nobody got from her was warmth and love, at least no outward display of it." When Louis was 8 years old the family moved to Chicago, where he would spend most of his life. From 1926 to 1936 his parents managed hotels that catered to blue collar workers, but included people from all walks of life. It was in those hotels, interacting with the tenants and guests and talking to people who gathered in nearby Bughouse Square, that Louis Terkel formed his understanding of humanity.

During this period in his life, Terkel attended the University of Chicago, receiving a degree in philosophy and subsequently graduating from that university's law school in 1934. After failing the bar exam he went to work for the Federal Emergency Relief Administration in Chicago and later for the U. S. Treasury Department in Washington, D.C. In 1938 he returned to Chicago and joined the Federal Writers Project.

His writing activity led him into acting with the Chicago Repertory Group, which resulted in his meeting Ida Goldberg, the woman he married in 1939. Their union lasted for sixty years until her death in 1999, and it produced one son, Dan. Also, from his acting came Louis Terkel's new name, "Studs," by which he would be known ever after. While performing in a play, the director of the play gave him that name to distinguish him from another actor who had the name Louis. Because Terkel was reading the novel *Studs Lonigan* at that time, the director decided to call him Studs, and the name stuck. Henceforth, there was no reference to Louis Terkel by him or others. He was Studs, permanently!

During the 1940s Studs Terkel had a short stint in the Army-Airforce and then hosted several radio shows until he was fired for political reasons. Because he signed and supported petitions for liberal and left wing causes he was bumped from his radio show by NBC, which caved in to pressures brought to bear as a result of the anti-communist crusade then being conducted by Senator Joseph McCarthy. Told by NBC that Terkel could keep his job if he admitted to being duped into signing the petitions, he refused, saying that admitting to being duped was the same as admitting to being stupid!

After being dumped from his radio program by a national network and being blackballed from commercial radio, Terkel went into theater for a time, touring the country as a cast member of "Detective Story," a popular play. Then one day, after months of being off the air, he contacted the WFMT radio station in Chicago and was put back on the air as "The Studs Terkel Program," a program that was heard daily for the next forty-five years, not ending until 1997. On it he interviewed a wide variety of guests, many of them prominent in American life, but he also interviewed police officers, convicts, nurses, loggers, former slaves, and former members of the Ku Klux Klan. He believed everyone had something worthwhile to say, and he was curious about everyone's story. He said he was curious all the time. On one occasion he said, "Curiosity never killed this cat—that's what I would like as my epitaph."

Simultaneously with conducting his radio show, he began making a name as a popular author, publishing his first book, *Giants of Jazz*, in 1956. This book was followed by numerous others on American history, books relying mainly on oral history. Among them were *Hard Times* and *An Oral History of the Great Depression*, both highly acclaimed. Yet, none was as successful as *The Good War: An Oral History of World War II*, which won for him the

Pulitzer Prize in 1985. One reviewer in 1985 characterized Terkel's work as "completely free of sociological claptrap, armchair revisionism, and academic moralizing." The author himself called his oral histories "guerilla journalism." More than anyone else, Studs Terkel transformed oral history into a popular art form. For his literary efforts, Terkel was elected in 1997 to the American Academy of Arts and Letters. Many other honors and awards were bestowed on him, including the George Polk Career Award.

As if being a radio, television, and literary celebrity wasn't enough, Terkel also played in several movies. Among the ones in which he had a role were "Eight Men Out," "Sacco and Vanzetti," and "Cheat You Fair: The Story of Maxwell Street."

In 2006 he joined a number of other plaintiffs in bringing suit against AT&T to prevent that telecommunications giant from giving customer telephone records to the National Security Agency without first getting a court order. Still smarting from being blackballed during the McCarthy era, Terkel protested against "using the telephone companies to create massive databases of all of our phone calls . . . ." The case was thrown out by federal Judge Matthew F. Kennelly. He ruled that what the government and AT&T were doing was necessary for the country's national security.

Terkel was in declining health when he stood up in 2006 for privacy rights. The year before, at age 93, he had under gone risky open-heart surgery. Even his doctors were amazed by his recovery. He not only recovered, but remained active. His last public appearance was in 2007. He announced that he was "still in touch—but ready to go." He gave his last interview on the BBC program 'Hard Talk" on February 4, 2008. He spoke of the impending election of Barack Obama to the presidency of the United

States, but he did not live to see that happen. He died at his Chicago home on October 31, 2008, at the age of 96.

I have already mentioned coming face to face with Studs Terkel in the home of Gene and Jeanne Sledge. That was the only time I ever saw him, but I did talk to him by telephone after that. Earlier I discussed the University of Montevallo's search for its featured speaker at the first Hallie Farmer Lecture Series. I noted that we were turned down by President Jimmy Carter, Madam Anwar Sadat, and Studs Terkel prior to offering an invitation that was accepted by Dean Rusk. Now, I reveal the details of the invitation to Terkel, the invitation that he declined to accept.

As chairperson of the committee to secure a speaker for the lecture series that we were establishing, I had to send a letter of invitation, written by me but signed by the school's president. I sent the required letter and heard nothing back from Terkel. Having been turned down by Carter and Sadat and hearing nothing from Terkel, I was getting a little uneasy about finding a "big name" speaker for our lecture series. I asked the president of the university, if he wanted to call Terkel, who had an unlisted number that we did not know. I said that Gene Sledge would probably have that number, if the president wanted to get it and call. The president looked a little sheepish at that suggestion, and told me to do it. I didn't know at the time that there was bad blood between Gene and the president. I knew that Gene didn't like him, but I did not know the depth of his animosity.

I called Gene, told him the situation, and asked if he would give me Terkel's number. He replied that he would do it for me, but that he wouldn't do "a damn thing" for the president. I didn't find out until later that the president had permanently alienated Gene by making fun of Gene's wife's heavy south Alabama accent. If you wanted to stay on Gene's good side messing with his family was one thing you did not do.

Anyway, Gene was kind enough to help me out with the number, and I called Terkel's office. He answered the telephone. I reminded him of who I was and where we had met and told him that we had sent him a letter five or six weeks earlier inviting him to be the first lecturer for the Hallie Farmer Lecture Series. I asked him if he got the letter. He said he had and that he meant to answer the "boy" who was president of the school, but that he just hadn't gotten around to it yet. "What's his name?" he asked me. I told him, and asked if he would do us the honor of coming for the event. "I don't think so," he said. "I'm too busy around here and don't think I can get away at this time. Tell him I can't come."

I expressed my disappointment about his rejection of our invitation and wished him a good day. As I hung up the phone, I thought, "If the president knew Terkel called him a boy and couldn't remember his name, he would have a conniption." Our president at that time was among the most narcissistic and pompous men I have ever known.

As it turned out, it was good that Terkel turned down the invitation to be the first Hallie Farmer lecturer at the University of Montevallo. If he had accepted, I would never have had the opportunity to meet and interact with Dean Rusk. I indicated above what a pleasure it was to be with Mr. Rusk. It would have been my loss, if I had not been privileged to get to know him. On the other hand, I had already been privileged to meet Studs Terkel and to follow that up later with the telephone conversation mentioned immediately above. Terkel was one of those rare people you meet once in a lifetime, and I am delighted that I had the opportunity to meet him.

Barbara Wertheim Tuchman

In the summer of 1970 the Morgans left the blistering heat of Bryan and College Station, Texas, for the cool breezes of New England. We had never been to Rhode Island, but I had the chance to be a visiting professor at Rhode Island College in Providence for the 1970-1971 academic year. What an opportunity! The colonial historian there, Evelyn Walsh, was slated to be on sabbatical, and I was invited to replace her while she was gone. Providence, Rhode Island, was a mecca for a colonial historian. After all, Brown University is there, and on Brown's campus is the John Carter Brown Library, one of the best places on earth for a colonial historian to do research. As fortune would have it, we were able to rent a furnished apartment on Hope Street, the apartment of another Rhode Island College faculty member, Sally Marks, who was also on sabbatical. Thus, we were able to take up residence not many blocks from Brown University. Indeed, it was within walking distance.

During the nine months we spent there, I was able to engage in research at the John Carter Brown Library one day a week. A side benefit was meeting some of Brown's outstanding faculty members—the eminent colonial historian Carl Bridenbaugh, the famous historian of American religion, William G. McGloughlin, and the future Pulitzer Prize winner, Gordon S. Wood. Gordon and I became friends, and he is one of the celebrities I met and will discuss below. Another historian I met was David Lovejoy of the University of Wisconsin, formerly of Brown University, who was on leave and also doing research at the John Carter Brown Library. It was David who introduced me to the famed Carl Bridenbaugh. Some of my professors at the University of North Carolina had spoken disparagingly of Bridenbaugh—one going so far as to say he had never met anyone who liked the man. I most assuredly wanted to meet this heralded historian, but I couldn't help wondering how he would receive me. To my delight, the great man was as kind as anyone could be. He treated me like an equal and not with the arrogance I expected from hearing about him.

Besides having the opportunity to do research in one of the world's premier libraries and getting to meet and have fellowship with several eminent historians, that year at Rhode Island College also brought me face to face with another famous writer of history—Barbara Wertheim Tuchman. I had read her widely acclaimed book, *The Guns of August*, but I had no way of knowing, of course, that spending nine months in Rhode Island would provide me with a chance to hear her speak and have a conversation with her. For the reader who might not know Tuchman's work, permit me to enlighten you.

Barbara Wertheim Tuchman was born in New York on January 30, 1912. She died on February 6, 1989, in Greenwich Hospital in Connecticut. She was born into a famous and wealthy family. Her father, Maurice Wertheim, was an investment banker, and her mother was Alma Morgenthau. Barbara's grandfather, Henry Morgenthau, Sr., was President Woodrow Wilson's ambassador to Turkey, and her uncle, Henry Morgenthau, Jr., was President Franklin D. Roosevelt's secretary of the treasury.

Needless to say, Barbara grew up with every advantage. She attended the best private schools and received her bachelor's degree from Radcliffe College in 1933. After her graduation from Radcliffe, she was a researcher in New York and Tokyo before turning to a brief career in journalism. She became an editorial assistant at *The Nation*, a magazine her father bought to keep it from going into bankruptcy. In 1937 she went to Spain to cover the Spanish Civil War for the magazine. Subsequently, she was a correspondent for the *New Statesman* in London.

In the midst of her journalistic career she married Lester Reginald Tuchman on June 18, 1940. Dr. Lester Tuchman was an internist who would later serve as a medical research professor of clinical medicine at Mt. Sinai School of Medicine. But first, there was World War II, and Dr. Tuchman did his part. He enlisted in the Medical Corps and was sent to Fort Rucker, Alabama. Barbara followed him there, but after he was sent overseas she went back to New York and got a job with the Office of War Information, preparing material on the Far East for use in broadcasts to Europe.

After the war Mrs. Tuchman began writing as much as she could. The fact that three daughters had been born to her and her husband limited her time for professional pursuits. Even so, she published her first major book in 1956—*Bible and Sword*—but it did not gain a great deal of attention. However, her second book, *The Zimmermann Telegram,* appeared two years later and was highly praised by Yale University diplomatic historian Samuel Flagg Bemis in the *New York Times.* At the time, Bemis was the foremost authority in his field.

Tuchman's greatest moment in the spotlight came because of her book *The Guns of August,* for which she won the Pulitzer Prize for Non-Fiction in 1963. Her research for this widely acclaimed book dealing with the onset of World War I included visiting the battlefields of France and Belgium, which she toured in a rented Renault sedan. She took notes on 4x6 index cards, because she said that they fit neatly into her purse and in shoe boxes. An oft-quoted passage from this outstanding work is: "Men could not sustain a war of such magnitude and pain without hope—the hope that its very enormity would insure that it would never happen again."

Tuchman followed winning the Pulitzer Prize in 1963 with a second one nine years later in 1972. Her second book to win this prestigious award was a biography of General Joseph Stilwell and was entitled *Stilwell and the American Experience in China, 1911-1945*. Next, she demonstrated her versatility by producing a book that had nothing to do with modern warfare. *A Distant Mirror*, published in 1980, was about 14th century France. It won the National Book Award in History.

In all of her books Tuchman practiced narrative history. Her writings are noted for attention to detail and a colorful style. She has been both lauded and criticized— always praised for a superb narrative and for making subjects come alive and for writing clearly about complex matters, while also being accused of "grave omissions" and "misinterpretations."

In spite of the fact that Tuchman never had an academic title or even a graduate degree, many honors were heaped upon her for her historical writings. She had honorary doctorates in literature from Yale University, Columbia University, New York University, Bates College, Williams College, and Smith College. She became a fellow of the American Academy of Arts and Sciences, and it awarded her the Gold Medal of History in 1978. She served as the academy's president, 1978-1980. During her final year as the academy's president, she was selected by the National Endowment for the Humanities to give the Jefferson Lecture, the federal government's highest honor for achievement in the humanities. The title of her lecture was "Mankind's Better Moments."

I cannot claim to have known Barbara Tuchman— only to have met her. She was a visiting speaker at Rhode Island College while I was a visiting professor there. In all honesty I don't remember much about her speech. What sticks in my mind was what she said about her writing habits. She said that she tried to write something every day, and some days she had trouble plowing ahead. On those days, she wrote perhaps no more than two hundred words. The next day she might be more inspired and write thousands of words, but it was important to her, she declared, that she make the effort to write something every day. Eventually, she said that it would all come together as a book. There was a reception for Tuchman following her talk, and I had the opportunity to greet her and have a brief conversation with her. As I recall, I told her that I loved *The Guns of August*. She thanked me, and we exchanged observations about our likes and dislikes in historical writing. I did not know at that time, of course, that she would soon come forth with a second Pulitzer Prize winner. Nor did I know that I would never read another of her books. It was not that I didn't like her work, because I loved her writing style. Rather, it was her subject matter that didn't interest me very much. Even though I read only one of her books and came to face to face with her only once, I still admire her contributions to historical writing and feel that I was privileged to have met this celebrity.

George C. Wallace

George C. Wallace, Jr., or "George C." as the family called him, more than any southern politician (except perhaps Huey P. Long) put the "P" in Populism and the "D" in Demagoguery. One writer noted after Wallace's death that he "strode the Alabama political stage like a colossus for over a quarter-of-a-century." No doubt he did, but he did it, according to Dan T. Carter, author of *George Wallace: The Politics of Rage*, by making a "Faustian bargain." Carter says of Wallace, "In order to survive and get ahead politically in the 1960s, he sold his soul to the devil on race." Wallace ultimately admitted as much, explaining his political ascendance this way, "You know, I tried to talk about good roads and good schools and all these things that have been part of my career, and nobody listened. And then I began talking about niggers, and they stomped the floor."

I met Wallace after he had become both famous and infamous. It was after he had been felled by a bullet from the gun of would-be assassin Arthur Bremer in 1972. In a wheelchair when I first saw him and met him, Wallace was governor of Alabama at the time. I was a new faculty member at the University of Montevallo, when the university's president invited the governor to come to our campus for a ceremony honoring him. The occasion was the naming of a new speech and hearing clinic building to be called "The George C. Wallace Speech and Hearing Clinic." Wallace arrived on campus with great fanfare and delivered a speech. He sat quietly on the stage smiling broadly until he was introduced. Rolled to the lectern, he was helped out of his wheelchair to his feet. As he stood up and grasped the lectern there was a thunderous applause from the audience. I cannot recall whether he was enabled to stand because of braces on his legs or by using crutches, but I do remember that he delivered his speech while standing. His address included some self-deprecating humor and some threats to send the federal government a message about states' rights. And, yet, Wallace didn't seem to mind taking federal money in the form of "revenue sharing," a program that President Richard Nixon had implemented. Indeed, the governor announced that he was going to share some of that revenue sharing money with the University of Montevallo for naming the speech and hearing clinic after him.

Before going any further regarding my personal encounters with George Wallace, I would like to provide the reader with some biographical information about him. He was one of four children born to George C. Wallace, Sr., and Mozell Smith Wallace. He began life in Clio, Barbour County, Alabama, on August 25, 1919. He grew up working on the family farm, and, like his parents, he was a Methodist.

Wallace became fascinated with politics around the age of ten, and at age sixteen he was chosen to be a page in the Alabama Senate. While serving in that capacity in Montgomery, he confidently announced that he would one day be governor of the state.

During Wallace's high school days he became a championship boxer in the bantam weight division. After his graduation in 1937, he bypassed college and went straight to law school at the University of Alabama in Tuscaloosa, and in 1942 he received his LL.B. degree.

Following his graduation from law school, Wallace entered pilot cadet training in the U. S. Army Air Corps, but he failed to win his wings. Upon washing out of the training program, he became a staff sergeant and a part of various crews that flew B-29 combat missions over Japan. While in the Air Corps he contracted a near-fatal case of spinal meningitis that left him with several disabilities. As a result he received a medical discharge with a disability pension.

Still fascinated with politics after he returned home from the war, Wallace ran for circuit judge in 1952 and was elected to Alabama's Third Judicial Circuit. He was viewed as a liberal judge. One black attorney said that Wallace was the first judge to call him "Mister" in an Alabama courtroom. Some have wondered if Wallace's granting probation to several black defendants caused him to be defeated when he ran for governor against John Patterson in 1958.

Wallace's loss to Patterson in that election was a watershed in his political career. He told an aide that he had lost because he had been "outniggered by John Patterson," and he vowed to "never be outniggered again." He never was. When he ran again in 1962, his rhetoric was laced with racist remarks and defiance of the federal government, and he won the election handily. He began his twenty-five years as the dominant figure in Alabama politics by saying in his inaugural address: "I draw the line in the dust and toss the gauntlet before the feet of tyranny, and I say segregation now, segregation tomorrow, and segregation forever."

From that point on Wallace became, as one writer has said, "the embodiment of resistance to the civil rights movement of the 1960s." During his first term as governor, the Barbour County native became known all over America for standing "in the school house door." He did it on television for the whole nation to see on June 13, 1963, personally barring the path of two black students, James Hood and Vivian Malone, who were trying to register for classes at the University of Alabama in Tuscaloosa. The governor was forced to step aside and let Hood and Malone register when President John F. Kennedy nationalized the Alabama National Guard, ordering the guardsmen to take charge of the situation. It is ironic that Wallace, as a delegate to the Democratic national convention in 1956, had suggested to fellow Alabama delegate Jimmy Sharbutt that they vote to nominate "that sailor" for president. That sailor, of course, was John F. Kennedy!

Wallace's defiance did not end in Tuscaloosa. Just three months after standing in the schoolhouse door there, he sent state police to Huntsville, Mobile, Tuskegee, and Birmingham to prevent public schools from opening after a federal court ordered the integration of Alabama schools. Civil disturbances followed, during which at least one person died. Again, President Kennedy nationalized the Alabama National Guard and forced the integration of the schools.

Racial violence abounded during Wallace's first term as governor. There were civil rights demonstrations in Birmingham in 1963, and Wallace sent state police to support the local authorities in their brutal suppression of the demonstrators. In March 1965 he ordered state police to Selma to assist local authorities there in stopping protestors who were demanding voting rights. The protestors clashed with the state and local police at the Edmond Pettus Bridge on "bloody Sunday" (March 7, 1965), when the demonstrators started their march toward Montgomery. The entire nation saw what happened at Selma, and this helped President Lyndon Johnson push the Voting Rights Act through Congress.

Wallace was elected governor three more times, and he ran unsuccessfully for president of the United States four times. In 1964, 1972, and 1976 he ran in the Democratic primaries seeking the Democratic Party nomination, but in 1968 he ran on his own American Independent Party ticket with retired Air Force General Curtis LeMay as his vice-presidential running mate. He got nearly ten million votes, or 13 percent of the total vote, and he carried five southern states and won forty-six electoral votes. Someone said that his campaigns were like "a one-man army going to war against the federal government."

In 1972 he once again became a candidate in the Democratic primaries, but his campaign faded away after he was shot. Even so, he won primaries in several southern states, plus the border state of Maryland and Michigan in the North. He tried again in 1976. He had little success and ended up endorsing the Democratic candidate, Jimmy Carter, who defeated incumbent President Gerald Ford in the general election.

Thus, by the time I met Wallace in 1973 or 1974 he was a well-known national figure. I recall speaking to him twice and corresponding with him once. He was never anything but cordial to me. On both occasions when I spoke to him, it was at luncheons held in his honor on the University of Montevallo campus. I told him who I was the first time, and he expressed pleasure at meeting me. We talked a little about the university. In general, we just made small talk. The second time I spoke to him, it was under almost exactly the same circumstances as the first time. I said, "Governor, I am sure you don't remember me from a year or so ago when we met. I am David Morgan, and I am on the faculty." He replied, "Oh, David, of course, I remember you." He followed that with words to the effect that he could never forget me and the great job I was doing at the university. All the time I was thinking, "Sure, Governor. I know you don't really remember, but it sure sounds good." Wallace had a genuine gift for making people feel good and feel like they were his personal friends.

I wish I could remember what happened on the occasion when I got a letter from the governor. It probably had something to do with my receiving a Certificate of Appreciation in 1976 for serving as chairman of the Alabama Bicentennial Celebration at the University of Montevallo. I seem to remember that the governor sent a letter thanking me for a job well done, but that was too long ago for me to be sure about the circumstances or the letter's contents. I just recall that I was surprised to get the letter and remember that it was filled with Wallace's usual flattering remarks.

George Wallace lived in pain for the last twenty-six years of his life. He died in Jackson Hospital in Montgomery on September 13, 1998, from septic shock caused by a severe bacterial infection. His son, George Wallace, III (but referred to as George Wallace, Jr.) and his daughter, Peggy Wallace Kennedy, were with him when he passed away. For good or bad, he was one of the giants of Alabama politics. I never voted for him for any office, governor or president, and I deplored his demagoguery. And, yet, I liked him personally, and admired him for saying that what he did in the 1960s to win elections was wrong. He went a long way toward making amends with the black community, even so far as to apologize to Alabama blacks for what he had done. He won a great many of them over. That was his great gift, winning people over. You might not like what he said he stood for, and he might not persuade you to vote for him, but if you met him, it was hard not to like him personally. I am glad I met him, and I did like him.

David Marshall "Carbine" Williams

My home town of Fayetteville, North Carolina, has seen many celebrities pass through it over the years— Franklin D. Roosevelt, Dwight D. Eisenhower, George C. Marshall, Amelia Earhart, Elvis Pressley, Joe Louis, Muhammad Ali, and Mickey Rooney—to name but a few of them. On the other hand, the town has produced very few celebrities, and the one most associated with it was actually born and reared in Godwin, a little town northeast of Fayetteville. He was a genius, a man who had an impact on World War II and, consequently, on the entire world. His name was David Marshall Williams, and his claim to fame is that he invented the short-stroke gas piston firing mechanism used in the M1 carbine. More than eight million American soldiers carried that weapon into battle during World War II, and, according to several top American generals, it played a significant part in our winning the war.

Although Williams ultimately achieved fame and fortune, he followed a checkered path to get there. Much of what follows about him comes straight from my book entitled *Murder Along the Cape Fear: A North Carolina Town in the Twentieth Century.* Mercer University Press published the book in 2005, and I am grateful to Dr. Marc Jolley, the press's director, for permission to repeat some of its contents here. I begin with the darker side of "Marsh" Williams, as he was called by family and friends, because he was infamous before he was famous.

Al Pate was reputed to be among the bravest and most popular deputy sheriffs in Cumberland County. A raid on a whiskey still made his wife a widow and his four children fatherless. On the night of July 22, 1921, Pate joined the county's sheriff, N. H. McGeachy, fellow deputy Bill West, and three other officers in a raid on a moonshine operation near Godwin, a few miles up the Cape Fear River on the opposite bank from Fayetteville. Upon the approach of the sheriff and his men, three men ran from the still. The six officers proceeded to confiscate the still and then drove off from the site carrying it in the sheriff's car. Shots rang out! The bullets barely missed the sheriff and West, while one struck Pate in the right side near the waist. As the bullet passed through, it severed a main artery. McGeachy took Pate to Dr. J. A. McLean, who informed the sheriff that his deputy had died immediately after being hit. From the doctor's office, McGeachy took Pate to Rogers and Breece Funeral Home, where he was to be prepared for burial.

This deputy sheriff was a well-loved man. The Reverend Joel Snyder performed his funeral service at the First Baptist Church, where Pate was a deacon. By all accounts his was one of the biggest funerals ever held in Fayetteville up to that time.

What of the man who shot him? That man, who was hardly more than a boy at the time, was David Marshall Williams, the son of J. Claude Williams, a former county commissioner. Young Williams was more than a little strange. His brother, the Reverend Mack Williams, was convinced that Marsh was insane and would testify to that at his trial. In retrospect, it is clear that Marshall Williams definitely marched to the beat of a different drummer. Though convicted of a murder he denied committing, Williams would spend nearly eight years in prison before being pardoned in 1929 by Governor Angus McLean. While an inmate he would invent the short-stroke gas piston firing mechanism that would later be used in the M1 carbine and that would ultimately earn him the nickname of "Carbine" Williams.

The famous actor James "Jimmy" Stewart would play this troubled genius in a 1952 movie based on Williams's life, "Carbine Williams." The world premiere of that movie was shown at the Colony Theater in Fayetteville, where I was an usher. I was there for that much ballyhooed event. I saw and spoke to Mr. Williams, the only time I ever did. He introduced me to his wife and his son David, as he entered the theater to watch the movie's premiere showing. Although Jimmy Stewart was not there for the occasion, actor Wendell Cory was. Cory played the part of "Captain Peoples," the warden who secured Williams' parole. I saw all of the hoopla. Williams spoke and introduced his wife and son to the audience. Cory spoke. What an occasion! I saw a real movie star close up; I saw a world-famous man who was hailed as a genius and a genuine hero. The movie, which I saw several times, was terrific. How could it have been anything else with Jimmy Stewart playing the leading role? To say the least, it was a dazzling experience for a fifteen-year-old boy. How could I have known then that some of it wasn't true? How could I have known that Hollywood had taken some of the liberties for which it is so notorious? Not until many years later did I discover the truth about David Marshall "Carbine" Williams.

Let me begin at the beginning. Marsh Williams was born on November 13, 1900, into a respected family near Godwin, a small town sitting near the east bank of the Cape Fear River between Fayetteville and Dunn. As a boy, Williams was fascinated with guns, building his first pistol at the age of ten. At his trial in 1921 family members testified that Williams had a history of doing crazy things with firearms. When Marsh was sent off to Blackstone Military Academy, he was soon in trouble for stealing guns and shipping the stocks home. He was expelled from the school. With misgivings he was allowed to marry in the hope that it would change him. When testifying at his son's trial in October, 1921, J. Claude Williams was asked why he had not gone to the authorities and reported some of the crazy actions of his son. Like any father, Mr. Williams said, he loved his son and hoped and prayed that he would change. Emotion overcame the distraught father, and he burst into tears. Even so, Mr. Williams denied knowing that his son was running a still and said he would have reported it to Sheriff McGeachy, if he had known. He also denied a report claiming that he said he would spend ten thousand dollars to get his son out of "killing Pate."

The events following the shooting of Deputy Al Pate (not federal agent Jesse Rimmer, as the 1952 movie had it) and leading up to the trial of Marshall Williams make a dramatic story. After Pate was killed, Sheriff McGeachy went to Williams' home and told his wife that her husband should give himself up. The next morning young Williams was handed over to the sheriff by his father and his uncle, Columbus McClellan. McGeachy took the suspect to "some unknown jail for safekeeping." About a week later Williams went before Recorder James C. McRae for a preliminary hearing. McRae denied the defendant bail and bound him over for trial before Judge John H. Kerr. J. Claude Williams immediately hired a legal firm from Dunn—John C. Clifford and N. A. Townsend—to defend his son. He soon added to the defense team Fayetteville attorneys John G. Shaw, Duncan Shaw, D. M. Stringfield, and V. C. Bullard. Marshall Williams' lawyers were judged by the press to be the "strongest array of legal talent this section of the state affords."

During the preliminary hearing it was noted that there was no eyewitness to the shooting, and thus the case was based on circumstantial evidence. The evidence included sworn and signed affidavits by Sheriff McGeachy and Randal (also known as "Ham") Dawson, a black man who had been at the still with Williams before the officers arrived on the scene. Dawson claimed that Williams admitted to him that he, Williams, had done the shooting and bragged that when he shot he didn't miss. Williams' black cohort said he was telling the truth "as certain as Jesus died." Both men were indicted by a coroner's jury. Pate's popularity prompted arguments for having the trial moved to another county so that the men could be sure of receiving a fair trial. That there was some cause for alarm is indicated by the fact that Williams was held until trial, not in the Cumberland County Jail, but in the Hoke County Jail in Raeford, some twenty miles west of Fayetteville. Even so, the trial was not moved out of Cumberland County.

The Williams defense team was up against a tough judge in John H. Kerr of Warrenton. When the judge addressed the grand jury on August 28, 1921, he said, "I cannot say what other judges will do, but for me, let them come before me on a second offense of toting pistols and other crimes, and they just as well kiss their wives and family goodbye, because I am going to send them away for a long time."

Williams' trial began on October 11, 1921. He was charged with first-degree murder. The strategy of Williams's lawyers was to argue that their client was insane and could not be held responsible for what he had done. A number of experts and "former school teachers" testified that Williams was "mentally unsound" and not responsible, if in fact he had shot Deputy Pate. Even family members made similar observations. J. Mack Williams, the preacher brother from Missouri, testified that he had warned his father, J. Claude Williams, in 1919 that Marshall was paranoid and might kill his father, mother, or wife, and burn the house down. "You are sitting on dynamite and don't know it," Mack warned the family physician, Dr. McLean. Also, Marshall Kornegay, Williams' maternal grandfather, claimed that insanity ran in the family. One of

Marshall's uncles, said Kornegay, had the same "mania" for firearms and finally killed himself with a shotgun.

All of these defense witnesses contradicted the experts from the State Hospital for the Insane, who had been put on the stand by the prosecutor. Those experts claimed that Williams was "subnormal" but that he definitely knew right from wrong. Dr. R. A. Allgood, the county coroner, asserted that Williams' intelligence was not up to that of "boys his age," but he certainly knew right from wrong.

The fate of Marshall Williams was handed to the jury on October 15, 1921. After forty-five hours of deliberation the jury hung at 11 to 1—eleven for sanity and one for insanity. Twelve for sanity would probably have landed Williams in the electric chair. As it was, a mistrial was declared. I was always told by my father that the man who hung the jury was Alton Spears, a man I knew from sometimes attending the Mt. Gilead Baptist Church. My father once told this to me in Mr. Spears' presence, and Mr. Spears did not deny it. I have no reason to doubt it, but I have no other confirmation that it is true.

With the mistrial, Williams was returned to the Hoke County Jail to see what the state would do next. When the state announced its intention for a retrial the next month before Judge Henry P. Lane, Williams pled guilty to second-degree murder and was sentenced to thirty years in prison. He left for state prison on the morning of Saturday, November 26. Sheriff McGeachy allowed Williams' father to accompany him and allowed Williams to stop by home and say goodbye to his wife and mother.

As for Ham Dawson, he was found not guilty, a decision that provoked Williams. He insisted that he did not shoot to kill, but Dawson did. According to the convicted man, he fired only once, while Dawson fired four times. Interestingly enough, the all-white jury believed the black man and not the white man in this case—a remarkable development in view of the fact that the Ku Klux Klan was being revived at that time and blacks were being lynched from time to time throughout the South. But Dawson went free, while Williams went to prison.

Less than eight years later Williams would walk away from the Caledonia Prison farm with a full pardon, thanks mainly to Captain H. T. Peoples, the warden at that prison location. In the meantime, he had resumed his interest in guns, inventing while incarcerated a breach-loading mechanism that would not jam. Some years later, on the eve of our entry into World War II, he used that mechanism when he built a demonstration model of what would soon become the M1 carbine. After working for a number of years for the Winchester Arms Company in Connecticut, he returned home to Godwin and continued his inventions until he ultimately held at least fifty patents. In 1971 his workshop was taken to the North Carolina Museum of History in Raleigh and put on display.

Marshall Williams was nationally famous by that time, but his health failed. Strokes took a toll on his body and mind. In 1972 he was admitted to Dorothea Dix Hospital in Raleigh, a facility for the mentally ill that was popularly known throughout North Carolina as "Dix Hill." There Williams died of pneumonia in January 1975, at age 74.

The Williams trial took place sixteen years before I was born, but I feel some connection with it because I knew some of the people who were involved in it. There was James McRae, the judge of Recorder's Court, who bound Williams over for trial. I knew of him nearly all of my life, and I knew his children, Jimmy and Betsy McRae. Betsy, as Elizabeth McRae, gained a measure of fame as Gomer Pyle's girlfriend on the Gomer Pyle television show. Judge McRae, as he was known when I first remember hearing of him, dispensed justice in Fayetteville for many years. Then, there was Alton Spears, whom I knew personally.

While I had no dealings with Williams himself, I saw and spoke to him on that one occasion in 1952 at the world premiere of the movie about him, and my uncle, Gilbert Herring (my mother's youngest brother), did have some dealings with him.

Uncle Gilbert fought in World War II in France, Germany, and Austria. When the war ended, he sent home a number of German rifles and shotguns. One of the shotguns, a sixteen gauge, was a fancy two-barrel shotgun with a .22 Hornet rifle barrel underneath the two shotgun barrels. There were two sights on the gun for use in shooting the .22 Hornet. One was a regular notched sight, while the other was a peep sight that lay on top of the gun in between the two shotgun barrels. It had to be flipped up for use. Not knowing quite how to sight the rifle barrel in, Uncle Gilbert told a friend, a deputy sheriff, about it. This friend, Deputy Archie Kitchens, happened to know Marshall Williams, or "Carbine," as nearly everyone was calling him by then. Kitchens suggested that Uncle Gilbert take the gun out to Marsh Williams and ask him what to do. My uncle said, "I don't really know Mr. Williams." The deputy volunteered to take my uncle to Williams' shop and introduce him. When they arrived there, Uncle Gilbert explained that he was not sure what to do about the sights for the .22 Hornet barrel. Almost without a word, Williams threw open a small window in front of his bench, pointed the gun at a target about thirty yards away from the shop, and using the notched sight, put a bullet in the dead center of the target. He then reloaded, flipped up the peep sight, and fired again. The second bullet struck a mere fraction to one side of the hole made by the first bullet. Williams then handed the shotgun to my uncle and said that the sights were just fine and that his advice was not to mess with them.

Uncle Gilbert had another occasion to be in Williams' presence. My uncle was a member of the FILI

(Fayetteville Independent Light Infantry), and "Carbine" Williams supported that independent military unit with financial contributions, fairly sizable ones, I have been told. On one occasion, the commander of the FILI decided to honor Williams for his support by holding a banquet and making the famous inventor the honored guest. The wine flowed freely at the banquet, and Williams became intoxicated. According to rumors, he was frequently intoxicated. After a number of glasses of wine, Williams apparently got bored with drinking, and when more wine was poured, he pulled out a .45 pistol and broke the glass, splattering the wine in all directions. Thinking that Williams wanted a different kind of wine, the commander of the FILI poured him a glass of a different variety. Again Williams pulled out his pistol and broke the glass, thereby making another mess. As a young man Williams had marched to a different drummer, and as an old man he obviously did the same.

My last connection with Marshall Williams, though he had long since gone to meet his maker, was in 2006. I went home to Fayetteville to speak before an audience at the Cumberland County Library on November 28 of that year. I was there to talk about my book, *Murder Along the Cape Fear: A North Carolina Town in the Twentieth Century.* One of Williams' nieces had taken umbrage at what I had written about her famous uncle. She tried to persuade the local newspaper not to publicize the event at the library. Of course, the newspaper ignored her, but she showed up at the presentation and told me that I should not have dredged up the past, because I had hurt her and her family. The audience was not sympathetic, one man stating that the past needed to be reported accurately, no matter who it might displease. Another man in the audience was a nephew or great nephew of Deputy Al Pate, whom Williams had killed. He was upset because the town considered Williams a hero. And so, long after his death in

1975, Williams remained a controversial figure—a hero to many and a murderer to some. To me he was a troubled genius who did a great service for his country, but at the same time a man who had a dark side. However he is looked upon, he remains arguably the most famous person and perhaps the only genius the Cape Fear region around Fayetteville has produced. I met him only once, but I feel like I know him well.

Gordon S. Wood

Gordon Stewart Wood is one of the most outstanding historians of our time. He is the only friend I have ever had who won the Pulitzer Prize. I have known him since 1970, and, though we have been in touch with each other only sporadically since I left Rhode Island in June 1971, I believe we have remained friends. Next to my colleague Gene Sledge, discussed earlier, I have come face to face with Gordon more than any of the other celebrities who have been treated in this book. Consequently, I am going to be very general in my presentation of Wood's life and career and focus more on the personal contacts I have had with him.

Gordon was born in Concord, Massachusetts, on November 27, 1933. I know little or nothing about his upbringing or early education. I only recently learned of his graduating summa cum laude from Tufts University in 1955. Although I have talked with him numerous times over the years, he has never mentioned anything about his early years—not his family, not his early education, nothing. Our conversations have included a lot of "shop talk," and, occasionally, we have discussed sports. Back in the days when we talked sports, he was a big fan of the Boston Celtics basketball team. He also mentioned to me how important it was to him to take care of family matters, but I never met his wife or any of his three children. Not surprisingly, two of his three children are history professionals, both teaching in universities.

Because I know so little of Gordon's personal life, I will focus my discussion of him on his professional life and career and on my personal experiences with him. He has been honored and won more awards than any historian I have known personally, and he has taught at some of the best institutions of higher education in America and Great

Britain. A list of his awards and publications is quite long, and so I will concentrate on the major ones, after mentioning his teaching career. While serving a stint in the United States Air Force in Japan he took his master's degree from Harvard University. After leaving the service he entered the Ph.D. program at Harvard, where he successfully attained his degree under the tutelage of Bernard Bailyn in 1964. He taught at Harvard while in graduate school and was then on the faculty at William and Mary College for two years (1964-1966). He returned to Harvard to teach for another year before going to the University of Michigan for two years. In 1969 he joined the faculty at Brown University, where he remained for the rest of his teaching career. However, he did accept visiting professorships at Cambridge University in England (1982-1983) and at Northwestern University (2001 and 2003).

If one includes the articles and reviews that Wood has contributed to professional and popular publications, the list is nearly as long as a football field. Rather than give a very long laundry list of those publications, I will highlight the significant books that won coveted prizes for him. In 1970 he won the prestigious Bancroft Prize for *The Creation of the American Republic*, a seminal study about the founding of our nation. Twenty-three years later, in 1993, he won the Pulitzer Prize for *The Radicalism of the American Revolution*, a controversial interpretation of that event, which provoked both praise and criticism. Another book, *Empire of Liberty: A History of the Early Republic, 1789-1815*, was nominated for the Pulitzer Prize in 2009 and was a finalist for that award. For these and other contributions to American historiography, Gordon received the National Humanities Medal in 2010. Clearly, Gordon Wood is one of the most celebrated historians of his generation and rightfully so.

I will now move on to my personal experiences with one of the brightest men I have encountered in my life's journey. As best I remember, I first met Gordon over coffee on the Brown University campus in the fall of 1970, and I believe that we were introduced by David Lovejoy, one of the most congenial people I have ever met. Some of the history faculty at Brown met for coffee each morning, and David encouraged me to join them. I got to know several of the history faculty members this way, including Gordon. We became friends, and this led, as I have said, to a lot of "shop talk" and to a discussion of professional basketball teams. I liked the Philadelphia 76ers at the time, because I knew Billy Cunningham, who was one of their star players. Gordon, who had spent years in Boston as a student and teacher, was a Celtics fan. I pulled for the Celtics, too, but not when they played against the 76ers. Gordon and I decided on one occasion to drive to Boston to see the two teams play against each other. We had a great time pulling for our respective teams. I think Boston won, but I am not sure. I do remember that Billy Cunningham had a good game and was clearly the outstanding player for Philadelphia that night. I recall that Gordon and I had pleasant conversations during the approximately hour's drive to Boston from Providence and on the return trip, but I can't remember a single thing that we talked about. I did not know, of course, that I was riding in the car of a future Pulitzer Prize winner and should be recording our conversations. At the time it appeared to me that we were just two friends who enjoyed watching and discussing a basketball game.

At the end of the 1970-71 academic year, I returned to Texas A&M University to resume teaching there. Two years later, in the summer of 1973, I left Texas and moved to Alabama to join the faculty of the University of Montevallo. Since my specialty in history is colonial America and the American Revolution, I was appointed chairperson of the University of Montevallo's Bicentennial Committee in 1976 to celebrate our nation's two hundredth anniversary. The first person I thought of as the perfect choice to bring to the campus to speak on the American Revolution was Gordon Wood. He accepted our invitation, partly because of our friendship and partly because he was also invited to speak at Huntingdon College in Montgomery, Alabama. He arranged it so that he could speak at both institutions during the same trip to our state.

I had read Gordon's book, *The Creation of the American Republic,* and, as so many others were, I was duly impressed. This rather sizable tome offers many brilliant insights into the founding of our country. Its size caused me to remark, when I introduced Gordon before he spoke to our university community, "Professor Wood's book reminds me of the editor who said of novelist Thomas Wolfe that he wrote books so big no one could even pick them up, much less read them." Everybody had a good laugh, even our featured speaker.

My mind wanders back to that time when Gordon visited our campus, and I recall that during our ride from the Birmingham Airport to Montevallo, he asked me a question about southern religious history and the sources that might be used to explain it. I told him what I thought might be the answer to the question, but I had to confess that I knew of no sources other than the ones that were well known. I added that I had explored the question pretty thoroughly, and that I had searched in vain for additional sources. His response made me feel good at the time and even better now. He said, "If you don't know, then I don't know anyone who does." Perhaps Gordon was giving me a bit too much credit, but it made me feel proud that he thought that.

At some point during his visit, we were walking across campus and encountered a woman who was one of my students. I spoke to her and introduced her to our distinguished guest. Then I said to her, "I saw you driving a new car a day or two ago. How do you like it?" I don't remember what kind of car it was, but I do recall that it was uniquely different from any design that the car maker had produced before 1976. I was curious about how well it was received by purchasers like my student. She said that she liked it very much, and we had a brief conversation about it. When we walked away from her, Gordon said, "I have noticed about Southerners that you are more interested in people and personal things than issues. You didn't ask her about her studies or what she thought about what you were covering in class. You were interested in her car." I guess Gordon's observation was right, at least in my case. When in class I usually focused on what I was teaching. Outside class, I was more interested in trying to connect with students on a personal level. I talked shop when I was in the shop, but engaged in very little professional dialogue when I saw my students outside that sphere. My recollection is that Gordon talked shop most of the time and, as he implied, he was issue oriented.

While he was in Montevallo to help us celebrate our nation's Bicentennial at the University of Montevallo, Gordon stayed at our residence on Brookhill Lane. On one of the evenings he was with us, Judy cooked dinner for Gordon and me, and we invited another guest to join us. She was Professor Lucille Griffith, my predecessor as chairperson of the Department of Social Sciences at the university. Lucille was a fine scholar in her own right. She, like Gordon and me, was a specialist in early American history and had written some noteworthy books on the colonial period. Her mentor at Brown University years earlier was one of Gordon's predecessors, another outstanding historian named Edmund S. Morgan. I asked Gordon earlier that day if he had ever met Lucille. He replied, "No, but I always wanted to. I am familiar with her work, of course." Three specialists in the same field of history can have a lot to talk about over dinner, but that night, which was a delightful occasion, I listened more than

I talked, as Gordon and Lucille discussed her work and his. They were complimentary of each other's contributions to our field of study.

When the Bicentennial celebration was over at our university, I drove Gordon to Montgomery to register at the Governor's House Motel, where the chairperson of Huntingdon College's Department of History had reserved a room for him. We said our goodbyes, and I didn't see Gordon again for seven more years. During the 1982-1983 academic year he was on leave from Brown University to serve as the Pitt Professor at Cambridge University in Cambridge, England. That is a visiting professorship that only a very few distinguished historians are invited to hold. It so happened that I took a tour group to the British Isles in 1983 to visit historic sites, and I wrote to Gordon that I was going over and would like to visit him at Cambridge. He agreed, and we arranged a time for me to see him. As I recall, my group reached London on Sunday afternoon, and very soon after our arrival I took the train to Cambridge and called him on the telephone. He picked me up at the train station in his car and escorted me around Cambridge University for several hours. The university consists of thirty-one colleges, and we had time to see his "rooms" at Gonville and Caius College (founded in 1348), after which we spent the remainder of the time we had together touring Trinity College (founded in 1546), perhaps the university's most prestigious college. It was fascinating to see up close one of the oldest and most famous universities of the Western World, and it was an added pleasure to be guided by a friend who was a distinguished guest lecturer there. When it was time for me to take the train back to London, Gordon let me off where he had picked me up. I did not know that I would probably never see my friend again. At least I haven't from then until now.

Although I have not seen Gordon since 1983, I have been in contact with him since then. In 1996 I had a book that was soon to be published—*The Devious Dr. Franklin, Colonial Agent: Benjamin Franklin's Years in London.* I wrote to Gordon and asked if he would write a blurb for the book's cover. He declined, saying that he had long ago resolved not to write blurbs for anyone, because such a policy eliminated "all sorts of problems." He wished me good luck with the book and said nothing about giving the book some publicity in another way. Then, a little later he wrote me a note saying that he was reviewing my book and another book, Robert Middlekauff's *Benjamin Franklin and His Enemies,* for the "The New York Review of Books." His last line read, "A review is better than a blurb any day." I wrote back and thanked him and then looked forward to reading the review, which appeared at approximately the time my book was available for purchase. I have always wondered if Gordon had already agreed to review the book and thought it inappropriate to tell me, or if he just wanted to surprise me. Whatever the case, he was right. No question about it! A review is better than a blurb any day, especially if the review is in such a distinguished publication as "The New York Review of Books" and by such an eminent scholar and Pulitzer Prize winner as Gordon Wood. And to make it even better, he had good things to say about my book and offered very little in the way of criticism.

That review appeared sixteen years ago. I have not been in touch with Gordon since then. We both retired from teaching soon after that, but in the years after 1996 Gordon has continued to receive high honors and much acclaim. I don't know how he is spending his retirement years, but I would be surprised if he is not working on another book or spending a great deal of time pondering momentous issues. I am glad that he and I became friends over forty years ago. Although I have had no contact with him since 1996, I believe that if I called him, learned that he is in good health, and proposed that we go to a Boston Celtics basketball game, he would be ready to go!

Conclusion

Besides these true celebrities who were famous or infamous, I met some other people along the way who were almost celebrities. Most of them were fellow historians who were in fact celebrities in our profession. Some of them achieved eminence in our field through books they wrote, while others made their marks as great teachers. For instance, Hugh T. Lefler, my mentor at the University of North Carolina at Chapel Hill, was known as "Mr. North Carolina History," both in North Carolina and throughout the South. Another of my professors, Fletcher Green, was said to have directed hundreds of master's theses and Ph.D. dissertations, and he accepted an invitation as a visiting professor at Oxford University in England. George B. Tindall of UNC contributed mightily to the historiography of the South through his publications. I was privileged to be his grader for a semester. Hugh F. Rankin of Tulane University wrote important books on the American Revolution and the Colonial period. I was privileged to be "one of his boys," as he called those of us who socialized with him at professional meetings. I also knew T. Harry Williams of Louisiana State University, a great writer on the Civil War. And there were Frank Vandiver of Rice University, also a friend, and John Belohlavek of the University of South Florida, a close friend and another great writer. I mentioned above Stephen Ambrose, whom I came to know when he delivered the Hallie Farmer Lectures at my university. I could probably think of others in my profession who deserve mention here, but I will mention just one more, Ben Procter of Texas Christian University, a close friend for nearly forty years.

Ben was a genuine character. Wherever he was, things happened. If at Educational Testing Service's Advanced Place reading in New Jersey, he put together ball games in the hours after the day's work was done. He organized trips to restaurants, lining up rides and telling people which car they were to ride in. The same thing happened at professional meetings. Ben would go around asking people if they wanted to join a party for dinner. Sometimes the parties became very large, but Ben always saw to it that people had a ride to and from the restaurant site. He loved to get people together more than anyone I ever knew. At the dinner gatherings, he saw to it that everyone present introduced himself or herself to the group.

Ben's background was unique, I think, for a historian. He was a star end on the University of Texas football team—indeed, an All American player. He caught passes for the legendary Bobby Lane. He became a professional player with the Los Angeles Rams for several years after graduating from the University of Texas, but when he was traded to the Washington Redskins and the coach proposed turning him into a defensive end, Ben would have none of it. "I catch passes," he told the coach. He threatened to leave the team, if the coach insisted on putting him at defensive end. Thinking that Ben was just another "dumb jock," the coach jokingly asked him what he would do if he left. Ben told him that he would go to Harvard University and get a Ph.D. degree in history. The coach apparently was skeptical of that, but Ben did leave. And he did go to Harvard and get his Ph.D. Then he embarked on a teaching career at Texas Christian University that spanned forty years. Along the way he wrote numerous books, important books—most of them on Texas history, but he is also heralded for a brilliant two-volume biography of William Randolph Hearst, the famous newspaper mogul. Also, during his teaching career, he directed the graduate work of dozens of students.

Ben enjoyed kidding people, especially people he liked, and he was a genuine prankster. I often said that the more he kidded you, the better he liked you. I remember one occasion when a group of us were discussing Billy the

Kid and the Lincoln County War. One of our group stated that one of his ancestors was involved in that famous event and that somebody had told him that he looked just like that ancestor in a picture the person had seen. Ben quickly said, "He must have been an ugly son-of-bitch." All of us had a big laugh, including the colleague whose ancestor had fought in the Lincoln County War.

Ben Procter died April 17, 2012, at age 85, and his passing was a great loss to me personally. It was my honor to be friends with Ben, his wife Phoebe, and their son Ben for so many years. My wife Judy and I still keep in touch with Phoebe, and we miss "the big guy" as so many of us called him.

There is one more almost-celebrity and friend whom I will mention in closing. He was a tennis friend that I knew for a number of years and came to know well during the last three or four years of his life. Like Ben, he was a genuine character, and he was as devoted to tennis as Ben was to teaching and writing history. His name was Don McDougal. I never saw Don play when he was at his peak, only when he was older and had stopped playing in tournaments sanctioned by the United States Tennis Association. He was a fierce competitor who had won countless tennis trophies, achieving high rankings at the state, regional, and even national levels. To my knowledge he was the only tennis friend I ever had who received two, free, new, tennis rackets every year from the USTA. He was entitled to them, because he had been ranked in the top twenty nationally. To him that was far more important than having been ranked number one in the South.

I played occasionally with Don when he lived northeast of Birmingham. We usually played at the Highland Park Racquet Club in Birmingham, and at our age we played doubles. Sometimes I played singles there, but never with Don, since he had given up singles altogether.

After the Pelham Racquet Club opened in 2000, I

started playing almost exclusively at that facility, and I lost touch with Don for several years. Pelham was only 15 miles from my house, while Birmingham was 35 miles away. One day (I am not sure of the year, but it must of have been 2005 or 2006.) I got a call from Don. He told me that he had just moved to Pelham and wanted to become involved in the tennis community there. Someone had told him that I knew all the players. "Get me into some doubles, David," he told me. I assured him I would try and believed I would have no trouble doing that. I promised to get back in touch with him soon. The last thing he said before hanging up was, "Don't forget me now." I told him that he would hear from me soon.

I got Don several matches and introduced him to many of the regular players. Within three weeks or a month he had taken over organizing men's doubles for the club, telling players the days they would play and what time of day. He warned that men who were scheduled to play needed to be there if the courts were playable, no matter what weather conditions were. Players who didn't fulfill their obligations to Don's satisfaction had to find some new partners. Although he was more than 75 years old, he played nearly every day.

Things changed for a time when Don's wife went out to Texas to visit relatives. She fell and broke a bone, was confined to a bed, and later went through rehabilitation for several months. Don left us to go out and help take care of her. I forget how long he was gone, but I am sure it was at least a full two months or more. When he returned, the first thing he told us all was that he did not want to resume being "captain." He was just going to be a regular player and not "run the show" anymore. That lasted about a week—two at the most.

Don was still "running the show" when he was 80 years old. I was off the courts from December, 2009, to April, 2010, with a second knee replacement. I had had my other knee replaced in 2001. I intended to work my way back slowly by playing one set each day for a few weeks. It was probably my second day back, when I played one set and was ready to call it a day. However, another player said he felt bad and had to quit. Don proceeded to tell me, "David, one of the players has to quit. It looks like you are going to have to keep on playing." I did. Why I did, I don't know, except Don told me I had to.

Don was a man of many tennis battles, some of them in relatively big matches. Never was there a fiercer competitor, and never was there an opponent who would congratulate you more quickly and graciously if you beat him fair and square. It was said of Don by some, "Even if you beat him, you won't be able to play your next match." That was because he would fight until the last point was over, and even if you won it, you would feel like you had been mauled by a lion.

In April 2010 Don was playing doubles with some of our regulars. This was just a week or so after he told me I had to continue playing in spite of my trying to make a slow comeback following knee replacement surgery. On this occasion he let several balls go by him without even moving his racket—something that was unheard of for him. He said he was having trouble seeing. He left the court, was taken to an urgent care place nearby and ultimately to an intensive care unit at a hospital. Having suffered a brain hemorrhage, he died two days later. A better script could not have been written for Don, except he would have wanted to die ON the court instead of being taken off of it. If he had lived until July 1, he would have turned 81. He was a professed atheist, prompting one of the members of our group, after he passed on, to say, "I don't know where Don is going, but as soon as he gets there he will reserve court number 4."

The two men I have discussed immediately above were colorful characters, fine men both of them. And they, too, were celebrities of a sort, especially in their limited spheres. Having known them means as much and perhaps a great deal more to me than crossing the paths of most of the celebrities I discussed earlier. In all cases, however, it was an enriching experience to meet all twenty of these people, even the ones I didn't like. We can learn from everyone we meet. We might not appreciate what they believe, do, or say, but knowing what they believe, do, or say broadens our perspective of the human race. I don't know if Will Rogers said he never met a man he didn't like or never met a man he couldn't like, but it was probably the latter. I, on the other hand, have met plenty of men and women that I didn't like and some that I don't think I COULD like, but I have learned much by rubbing shoulders with the celebrated and the uncelebrated. I am pleased that I had the opportunity to meet a few of the celebrated and to discover that most of them deserved the acclaim they received from their fellow human beings.

Finis

Other Paperback and Kindle Books

by

David T. Morgan

1. *Acrimony in a Little Corner of Academia,* 2011.
   Order the paperback at
www.createspace.com/3586551 or the Kindle version at
www.amazon.com/dp/B0051BE586. Borrow it free from
the Kindle Library.

2. *Ireland, Poor Ireland: A Dangerous Man and the
   Woman He Adored,* 2012.
   Order the paperback at
www.createspace.com/3803846 or the Kindle version at
www.amazon.com/dp/B007MRNWTK. Borrow it free
from the Kindle Library.

Books available from www.amazon.com

*The New Brothers Grimm and Their Left Behind Fairy
Tales,* 2006.

*Murder Along the Cape Fear: A North Carolina Town in
the Twentieth Century,* 2005.

Southern Baptist Sisters: In Search of Status, 1845-2000,
2003.

*The Devious Dr. Franklin, Colonial Agent: Benjamin
Franklin's Years in London,* 1999.

The New Crusades, the New Holy Land: Conflict in the Southern Baptist Convention, 1969-1991, 1996.

Books available from www.lulu.com/spotlight/morgan70

A Blue Voice Crying in the Wilderness of a Red State, 2009.

America's Revival Tradition and the Evangelists Who Made It, 2008.

The Righteous and the Mighty, 2009.

Books available from www.authorhouse.com

Spiritual Spokesmen of the Ages: The Men Who Inspired the World's Major Religions, 1998.

The New Great Wall, 1999.

About the Author

David T. Morgan, a professional historian, spent thirty-three years in the college classroom before retiring in 1997. Twenty-four of those years were spent at the University of Montevallo in Montevallo, Alabama He holds the B.A. degree in history from Baylor University and M.A. and Ph.D. degrees in history from the University of North Carolina at Chapel Hill. He was national president of Phi Alpha Theta, the national history honor society, in 1998-1999. He is author of numerous professional articles and more than a dozen books. His books include works of history, religion, and fiction. A number of those books are available for purchase and listed above.

The author currently lives in Alabama with Judith McIntosh Morgan, his wife of 54 years. They have two grown children, Cindi Reeves and Brian Morgan, and two grandchildren, Matt Reeves and Riley Paige Morgan.

18205213R00071

Made in the USA
Charleston, SC
22 March 2013